THE
HUMBLE
CRUMB

Soups, sauces, pâtés, puddings, casseroles and cakes . . . food for all the family – and a concern for the needs of the world.

Faced with the cries of the world's poor, Elizabeth Jones found herself unable to throw away the left-over crusts from her kitchen. Surely a jar full of humble crumbs could be made into a nutritious and enjoyable family meal?

So began this collection of over 200 recipes. Many are based on traditional home cooking from a less throwaway age. All arise not only from the author's concern with food for the family but also for others. From soups to sweets, each one of these dishes is made with the same underrated ingredient: breadcrumbs.

THE
HUMBLE
CRUMB

Elizabeth Jones

Illustrations by
Peter Bailey

A LION PAPERBACK

Oxford · Batavia · Sydney

Published by
Lion Publishing plc
Sandy Lane West, Littlemore, Oxford, England
ISBN 0 7459 1564 7
Albatross Books Pty Ltd
PO Box 320, Sutherland, NSW 2232, Australia
ISBN 0 7324 0005 8

First published 1989

British Library Cataloguing in Publication Data

Jones, Elizabeth
  The humble crumb
  1. Food. Dishes using breadcrumbs.
  Recipes
  I. Title
  641.6'31

  ISBN 0-7459-1564-7

Printed and bound in Great Britain by
Cox and Wyman Ltd, Reading

CONTENTS

NOTES

Metric and imperial measurements have been calculated separately. Use one set of measurements only as they are not exact equivalents.

Always pre-heat the oven or grill to the specified temperature.

Cooking times may vary slightly depending on the individual oven. Dishes should be placed in the centre of the oven unless otherwise specified.

INTRODUCTION

*The land produced vegetation: plants
bearing seed according to their kinds
and trees bearing fruit with seed in it
according to their kinds. And God saw
that it was good.*

Genesis 1:12

We see and hear so much today of children in
the Third World who are poor and starving.
Meanwhile we, in the so-called wealthier
nations, do not consider ourselves to be wealthy
at all. We hear of pensioners struggling to make
ends meet. Young people, despite their educa-
tion, are unable to find employment equal to
their talents. Middle-aged executives become

redundant in the prime of their lives. One-parent families and widows struggle to manage on reduced incomes. We consider ourselves to be poor.

But . . . are we? At any time we can go to the supermarket and pick up a loaf. No one is so poor that they cannot at least buy bread. We even throw away crusts and stale bread. In this context we must consider ourselves, irrespective of what category we are in, to be very rich indeed. We can thankfully say that our children and grandchildren are not dying of malnutrition. So what can we do about the starving millions?

Our nations are spending annually large amounts of money trying to help. Statistics show that the numbers of poor in the world are increasing year by year. We ask ourselves, 'What can we do?', but allow the problem to remain in the back of our minds. We see item after item of news, of sick and hungry children who are fighting for survival in Ethiopia, Eritrea, Chad and the Sudan, the list growing longer all the time. But how soon we forget . . .

Pope John Paul II, in one of his Easter messages from the Vatican, said, 'The health of the whole world must be the concern of us all.' While I was watching a church service on television, a minister, praying, said, 'King of the universe who brings forth bread, help us to appreciate and not to waste.' Listening to these men of God made me feel very guilty the next time I came to throw away stale bread. 'But what good is a chunk of stale bread?' I asked myself. Pope John Paul's pleading voice, 'I beg of you, I implore you, I beg on bended knee,' echoed through my mind. So my bread was broken into small pieces, popped into the electric blender, and with no effort on my part I had a basin full of breadcrumbs. With a pinch of sage, a few dried onion rings, seasoning and a little boiling water, I had some delicious sage and onion stuffing for my chicken. It was almost as simple to make as any of the packet variety, and I was proud of myself for not wasting that piece of bread.

A few days later I found myself with some more crusts that nobody in my family would eat. These, too, were turned into breadcrumbs. Then I found myself asking, 'What am I going to do with all these?' The stale bread kept turning up and I exchanged the bowl for a larger one. I had heard that there was a growing mountain of butter in Europe, and I began to envisage a mountain of breadcrumbs appearing in my kitchen! I thought (usually in the middle of the night) about these breadcrumbs and decided what I would do with them. The next day I began to experiment. I remembered some of my grandmother's recipes, my mind having stored from childhood little bits of information which I had never given a thought to before. As these experiments began to turn out successfully, I became very bold in all manner of dishes. The mountain of breadcrumbs was now being used up daily.

I convinced myself that these recipes were a simple exercise in the reduction of waste, but soon found myself on several occasions stealing fresh bread to turn into breadcrumbs to make a meal go further. I began to feel like the widow we read about in the Bible, whose barrel of flour never ran out (1 Kings 17:16). I had a constant bowl of breadcrumbs, which were costing me nothing. The birds in my garden must have wondered what had happened!

The recipes in this book all started with a teacupful of breadcrumbs, which I found convenient, quick and simple, using the same size teacup all through the recipe. For the purposes of this cookbook, they have been converted into grams and ounces. The breadcrumbs used were sometimes white and sometimes brown, but mostly mixed, as we eat both white and wholemeal bread, and they all worked. I was very pleasantly surprised to see the versatility of the humble crumb.

I am not quite sure how my humble effort will help the hungry people of the world, but it's a start. We can *all* do something to show our concern to reduce waste from our cooking and to turn our hearts to God in thanks for providing for all our needs.

Elizabeth Jones

SAUCES AND STUFFINGS

To God, who gives our daily bread
A thankful song we raise,
And pray that he who sends us food
May fill our hearts with praise.

Thomas Tallis

APPLE SAUCE

100 g (4 oz) breadcrumbs
175 g (6 oz) sugar
450 g (1 lb) large cooking apples
1 egg
nutmeg
butter or margarine

Peel, core, and slice the apples. Place in a saucepan with a knob of butter or margarine, and a very little water, and cook until tender. Add the sugar and a pinch of grated nutmeg. Stir until the sugar dissolves.

Beat the egg and stir in with the breadcrumbs. Leave to cool. Serve with pork or goose.

Try using a different spice, such as cinnamon or allspice, in each batch. This recipe freezes well in small margarine pots for use as required.

APRICOT AND WALNUT STUFFING

100 g (4 oz) breadcrumbs
1 medium onion, finely chopped
50 g (2 oz) shelled walnuts, chopped
50 g (2 oz) dried apricots, chopped
1 teaspoon salt
½ teaspoon parsley, chopped
pinch of pepper

Place the breadcrumbs in a mixing bowl, add the onion, the apricots and walnuts, salt, pepper and parsley and mix together. Add a little boiling water to bind together.

This stuffing is delicious if you remove the bone from a shoulder of lamb, filling the cavity with the mixture. If preferred, cook in a buttered ovenware dish at the same temperature as the meat, removing when cooked. Keep warm until ready to serve.

BREAD SAUCE

75 g (3 oz) breadcrumbs
1 medium onion, peeled
1 tablespoon butter
600 ml (1 pint) milk
2 cloves
1 bay leaf
salt and pepper

Press the cloves into the onion and place with the bay leaf in a saucepan with the milk. Bring to the boil. Add the breadcrumbs and simmer gently for 20 minutes.

Remove the bay leaf, onion and cloves. Add the butter and salt and pepper to taste. Beat well together. Serve with meat or poultry.

CELERY AND ONION STUFFING

100 g (4 oz) breadcrumbs
2 sticks celery, finely chopped
1 small onion, finely chopped
1 teaspoon parsley, chopped
1 egg
salt and pepper

Place the breadcrumbs, celery, onion, parsley and seasoning in a mixing bowl. Beat the egg and mix in well, adding a little water to bind together.

This stuffing is very tasty served with beef or lamb. Cook separately in a buttered ovenware dish or press into crevices in boned lamb or rolled beef.

CHESTNUT STUFFING

100 g (4 oz) breadcrumbs
100 g (4 oz) chestnuts
1 small onion, chopped
1 teaspoon parsley, chopped
salt and pepper

Pierce the chestnuts with a sharp knife and boil in water for 20 minutes. Shell them and chop them up roughly. Mix in with the breadcrumbs, onion, parsley, salt and pepper to taste. Add a little boiling water to bind together.

This stuffing is excellent with poultry.

FORCEMEAT STUFFING

50 g (2 oz) breadcrumbs
1 tablespoon suet
1 tablespoon parsley, chopped
1 egg, beaten
1 lemon rind, finely grated
¼ teaspoon mixed herbs
salt and pepper

Mix together the breadcrumbs, suet, parsley, lemon rind, herbs and seasoning. Bind together with the egg.

An excellent stuffing for game, poultry or veal.

GOOSEBERRY SAUCE

100 g (4 oz) gooseberries
50 g (2 oz) breadcrumbs
120 ml (4 fluid oz) water
1 tablespoon sugar
butter or margarine
nutmeg

Cook the gooseberries in the water until soft. Remove from the heat and add the sugar, a knob of butter or margarine, a pinch of nutmeg and the breadcrumbs. Mix well, then pass all through a wire sieve.

Reheat and serve hot with mackerel.

HAM AND MUSHROOM STUFFING

50 g (2 oz) breadcrumbs
50 g (2 oz) mushrooms, chopped
100 g (4 oz) ham, chopped
1 teaspoon parsley, chopped
1 small onion, chopped
thyme
cooking oil
salt and pepper

Mix together the breadcrumbs, mushrooms, ham, onion and parsley with a pinch of thyme and a little salt and pepper. Fry gently in a little hot oil for 10 minutes.

This is a tasty filling for marrow, tomatoes, green peppers or onions. Slice the top off the vegetables, de-seed them, and fill the hollow with the stuffing. Place in an ovenware dish with a little water. Dot with butter and bake in a moderate oven (Gas Mark 4, 350°F, 180°C) for about 30 minutes. Serve with curried rice.

LEMON AND THYME STUFFING

100 g (4 oz) breadcrumbs
1 small onion, finely chopped
$\frac{1}{2}$ lemon
1 teaspoon thyme
salt and pepper

Place the breadcrumbs in a mixing bowl and add the onion, thyme and lemon juice. Grate the rind off the lemon and add to the mixture. Add a little salt and pepper and mix well, binding all together with a little hot water.

This stuffing is particularly good with roast duck.

Orange Stuffing

175 g (6 oz) breadcrumbs
finely grated rind and juice of 1 orange
1 medium onion, finely chopped
1 dessertspoon parsley, finely chopped
1 level teaspoon salt

Pour the orange juice onto the breadcrumbs in a mixing bowl. Add the orange rind, chopped onion, parsley and salt to this mixture. Mix well together, adding a little boiling water to bind.

This tangy stuffing is excellent cooked with pork.

PRUNE AND APPLE STUFFING

2 large cooking apples
50 g (2 oz) breadcrumbs
225 g (8 oz) cooked prunes
1 dessertspoon sugar
1 tablespoon water
1 teaspoon lemon juice
salt and pepper

Peel and core the cooking apples and cut up into slices. Cut the cooked prunes in two and remove the stones. Add the breadcrumbs and sugar to the fruit with the lemon juice, a little salt and pepper and the water. Mix all together.

Excellent if spooned into a duck, roasted in a hot oven, and served dressed with watercress.

Sage and Onion Stuffing

50 g (2 oz) breadcrumbs
1 teaspoon dried onions
$^1/_2$ teaspoon dried sage
salt and pepper

Mix together all the dry ingredients in a basin. Add a little boiling water. Cover with a plate and leave to soak for a few minutes.

This makes a tasty stuffing for poultry or pork.

Sausage Stuffing

50 g (2 oz) breadcrumbs
225 g (8 oz) sausagemeat
1 egg, beaten
1 teaspoon parsley, chopped
$1/4$ teaspoon mixed herbs
salt and pepper

Mix together all the ingredients, binding with the beaten egg.

A useful alternative to sage and onion, this stuffing is particularly good if cooked inside a chicken.

SOUPS

God, our Maker, doth provide
For our wants to be supplied:
Come to God's own temple, come,
Raise the song of harvest-home.

Henry Alford

CELERY SOUP

50 g (2 oz) breadcrumbs
175 g (6 oz) potatoes, peeled and diced
450 g (1 lb) celery, chopped
175 g (6 oz) onions, chopped
1 dessertspoon dripping or vegetable oil
1 tablespoon celery leaves, finely chopped
1 chicken stock cube
1 litre (2 pints) water
salt and pepper

Place all the ingredients except the celery leaves in a pressure cooker. Cook at 15 lb pressure for 30 minutes. Turn off the heat and leave to cool slowly.

Chop the celery leaves finely, and reserve.

When the soup has cooled, pour into a liquidizer or blender a little at a time and process until smooth. Pour into a saucepan. Add the celery leaves and bring to the boil. Turn down the heat and simmer for a further 5 minutes before serving.

Serves 4-6

CHICKEN BROTH

50 g (2 oz) breadcrumbs

1 large onion, chopped

1 large carrot, chopped

1 large leek, chopped

175 g (6 oz) tomatoes, chopped, or 1 x 400g (14 oz) tin tomatoes

175 g (6 oz) mixed dried peas and beans

1 litre (2 pints) water

1 teaspoon salt

1 teaspoon paprika

$^1/_4$ teaspoon pepper

1 chicken stock cube

1 chicken carcass

chicken giblets

Place the bones and giblets of a chicken in a pressure cooker with the water. Cook for 30 minutes at 15 lb pressure. Allow to cool, then pour through a sieve.

Add to the soup the other ingredients and a little more water, if required. Simmer gently for 1 hour, stirring occasionally. This recipe makes a good thick broth.

Serves 4-6

GREEN PEA SOUP

1 bacon shank
50 g (2 oz) breadcrumbs
175 g (6 oz) split peas
1 large onion, chopped
2 carrots, chopped
$\frac{1}{2}$ teaspoon parsley, chopped
$\frac{1}{4}$ teaspoon allspice (optional)
$1\frac{1}{2}$ litres (3 pints) water
pepper

Soak the bacon overnight in cold water to remove salt. Pour away the water, then place in a saucepan and cover with 2 pints of fresh water. Bring to the boil, then lower the heat and simmer for 2 hours, removing any scum that comes to the top.

Remove bacon from the pan and add all the other ingredients to the stock except the parsley. Simmer with the remaining water for about 40 minutes.

Cool slightly before passing through a wire sieve or blender. Return to the saucepan with the chopped parsley and reheat before serving.

Serves 6

LEEK AND POTATO BROTH

50 g (2 oz) breadcrumbs
6 medium potatoes
3 or 4 leeks
120 ml (4 fluid oz) evaporated milk
1 litre (2 pints) chicken stock
salt and pepper

Wash and clean the leeks thoroughly and chop finely. Peel and slice the potatoes and place them in a saucepan with the breadcrumbs and chicken stock. Cook until the leeks are tender.

When cool, pass all through a blender. Return to a low heat and add evaporated milk, salt and pepper to taste.

This broth is good and hearty, and is excellent served with fresh crusty bread.

Serves 4-6

LEEK AND TOMATO BROTH

50 g (2 oz) breadcrumbs
1 medium carrot, chopped
1 medium onion, chopped
350 g (12 oz) leeks, sliced
1 x 400 g (14 oz) tin of tomatoes
small pinch of oregano
salt and pepper
3 beef stock cubes
water

Place all the ingredients in a large saucepan covering with water before adding the tomatoes. Bring to the boil, adding salt and pepper to taste. Lower the heat and allow to simmer for 45 minutes.

Serve this tasty broth with hot buttered toast.

Serves 4-6

MUSHROOM SOUP

50 g (2 oz) breadcrumbs
225 g (8 oz) mushrooms, chopped
4 good mushroom tops
1 medium potato, peeled and diced
1 medium onion, chopped
1 medium carrot, chopped
1 tablespoon cooking oil
1 teaspoon yeast extract
1 litre (2 pints) water
salt and pepper

Pour the cooking oil into the base of a pressure cooker. Add the chopped mushrooms and onions and fry gently, stirring frequently.

Mix the yeast extract into the water, making two pints of stock. Pour into the pressure cooker and add all the remaining ingredients except the four good mushroom tops. Cook for 30 minutes at 15 lb pressure.

Leave to cool, then liquidize and transfer to a fresh saucepan. Take the four uncooked mushroom tops and slice very thinly. Add to the soup and bring to the boil. Lower the heat and simmer for 5 minutes before serving.

Serves 4-6

ONION SOUP

50 g (2 oz) breadcrumbs
2 large onions, chopped
50 g (2 oz) butter or margarine
1 litre (2 pints) water
50 g (2 oz) grated cheese
bread rings
vegetable oil

Melt the butter or margarine in a saucepan and add the onions. Cook with lid on pan at a very low temperature for 30 minutes, stirring occasionally.

Add the breadcrumbs, water, salt and pepper to taste. Continue cooking for another 30 minutes.

Allow to cool, and pass through a wire sieve or blender. Pour into a heat-proof soup tureen and place in a moderate oven to warm through.

Cut slices of stale bread into rings with a pastry cutter and fry in hot oil until golden brown. Drain well on kitchen paper and place on top of the soup. Sprinkle with grated cheese. Pop the tureen under the grill for a few minutes to cook the cheese before serving.

Serves 4-6

SCOTCH BROTH

1 marrow bone
50 g (2 oz) breadcrumbs
1 large onion, chopped
1 large carrot, chopped
50 g (2 oz) swede, chopped
1 leek, chopped
50 g (2 oz) dried peas
50 g (2 oz) dried beans
100 g (4 oz) barley
1 x 400 g (14 oz) tin tomatoes
2 beef stock cubes
dash of Worcester sauce
salt and pepper

Ask the butcher for a chopped marrow bone. Wash well in salted water before placing in a pressure cooker. Cover with water and simmer for 2 hours. Remove the bones and strain the liquid into a bowl. Leave overnight in the refrigerator. Remove the fat and pour the stock into a large pan. Add all the other ingredients and simmer for 1 hour, adding more water as required. This makes a delicious and nourishing thick broth.

Serves 4

TOMATO SOUP

50 g (2 oz) breadcrumbs

1 medium onion, sliced

1 medium carrot, diced

1 litre (2 pints) water

1 dessertspoon dripping or cooking oil

salt and pepper

1 x 125 g (5 oz) tin tomato purée

150 ml (5 fluid oz) milk

1 dessertspoon sugar

Pour the water into a pressure cooker and add the breadcrumbs, onion, carrot, dripping or oil, salt and pepper to taste. Cook at 15 lb pressure for 30 minutes. Allow to cool, then pass through a wire sieve or blender.

Transfer to a fresh pan and add the tomato purée and sugar. Bring to the boil and add the milk. A sprinkling of finely chopped parsley or chives makes a good garnish for this very tasty soup.

Serves 4-6

Pâtés and Spreads

All things living he doth feed,
His full hand supplies their need:
For his mercies shall endure,
Ever faithful, ever sure.

John Milton

CHICKEN PÂTÉ

100 g (4 oz) breadcrumbs
180 ml (6 fluid oz) water
175 g (6 oz) lamb's liver
175 g (6 oz) bacon pieces
1 plump chicken leg
1 chicken heart, liver and gizzard
1 teaspoon salt
pinch of pepper
1 teaspoon lemon juice
½ teaspoon sage

Place the liver, bacon, chicken and giblets in a pressure cooker. Pour over the water, lemon juice, herbs and seasoning, and cook for 15 minutes at 15 lb pressure. Turn off the heat and allow to cool down slowly.

Remove the bones from the chicken then liquidize the meat with a little of the liquid. Mix well into the breadcrumbs and place in a straight-sided ovenware dish. Cover with baking paper and tie down. Stand the dish in a tray of water and cook for 2 hours in a hot oven (Gas Mark 6, 400°F, 200°C).

Remove chicken pâté from the oven and cover with a plate. Leave to cool, then store in the refrigerator.

DUCK PÂTÉ

175 g (6 oz) breadcrumbs
180 ml (6 fluid oz) water
4 rashers bacon, chopped finely
1 large orange
1 teaspoon grated orange peel
leg, breast and giblets of a duck
salt and pepper

Cut enough meat off the duck breast to make up to 1 lb in weight with the leg. Place in a pressure cooker, adding the liver, heart, gizzard and bacon. Halve the orange and cut off one thin slice to be used as a garnish. Add the juice of the orange and the finely grated peel. Add the water and cook in a pressure cooker for 15 minutes at 15 lb pressure. Turn off the heat and leave to cool slowly.

Remove the bones then liquidize the mixture. Add the breadcrumbs, salt and pepper to taste and mix together well. Spoon into a straight-sided dish. Press on the orange slice. Cover with baking paper and tie down. Stand the dish in a tray of water and cook for 2 hours in a hot oven (Gas Mark 6, 400°F, 200°C).

Remove duck pâté from the oven and cover with a plate. Leave to cool, then store in the refrigerator.

KIPPER TOAST SPREAD

175 g (6 oz) cooked kipper

1 tablespoon cream or natural yogurt

1 tablespoon butter or margarine

$^1/_2$ tablespoon parsley, chopped

25 g (1 oz) breadcrumbs

Carefully remove any bones from the cooked kipper, then pass through a mincing machine or blender.

Melt the butter or margarine in a saucepan, add the cream or yogurt, kipper and breadcrumbs. Stir until all are well blended and cook for 2 minutes.

Serve spread on hot buttered toast.

LIVER AND BACON PÂTÉ

50 g (2 oz) breadcrumbs
100 g (4 oz) pig's liver
100 g (4 oz) bacon
50 g (2 oz) red peppers, chopped
$\frac{1}{2}$ teaspoon garlic paste
210 ml (7 fluid oz) water
salt and pepper

Chop the meat and add to a pressure cooker with the water, garlic paste, finely chopped peppers and salt and pepper to taste. Cook for 15 minutes at 15 lb pressure. Allow to cool, then liquidize before mixing in the breadcrumbs. Put in a straight-sided ovenware dish, cover with baking paper and tie down. Stand the dish in a tray of water and cook for 2 hours in a hot oven (Gas Mark 6, 400°F, 200°C).

Remove the liver and bacon pâté from the oven, and cover with a plate. Leave to cool, then store in the refrigerator.

MACKEREL PASTE

50 g (2 oz) breadcrumbs
225 g (8 oz) smoked mackerel
1 dessertspoon sunflower oil
juice of ½ lemon
black pepper
melted butter

Skin the mackerel and remove any bones. Break into small pieces and place in a mixing bowl. Add the breadcrumbs, sunflower oil, the juice of half a lemon and a sprinkling of freshly ground black pepper. Mix together before spooning into a blender or food processor. Process until it forms a smooth paste. Spoon into a suitable container and pour over the top a little melted butter.

This will keep well in a freezer or for days in a refrigerator. It is delicious spread on hot toast.

MINCE COLLOPS

50 g (2 oz) breadcrumbs
450 g (1 lb) cold cooked beef, finely minced
25 g (1 oz) dripping or 1 tablespoon vegetable oil
1 medium onion, finely chopped
1 dessertspoon tomato purée
600 ml (1 pint) water
salt and pepper

Heat the dripping or oil in a saucepan and add the beef and the onion. Stir over the heat until the onion has browned. Add the water and cook for 15 minutes. Add the tomato purée, breadcrumbs, salt and pepper to taste and continue cooking for a further 15 minutes.

Serve this meaty, coarse pâté very hot with fingers of hot toast. Leftovers make a tasty sandwich filling.

MUSHROOM PÂTÉ

100 g (4 oz) brown breadcrumbs

1 tablespoon cooking oil

175 g (6 oz) button mushrooms, thinly sliced

50 g (2 oz) onion, finely chopped

1 small carton natural yogurt

generous pinch of salt

black pepper

Pour the oil into a frying pan and heat. Add the mushrooms and the onion, and sprinkle the salt over this mixture. Sauté, stirring constantly with a wooden spoon. Remove from the heat and allow to cool.

Add the breadcrumbs to the mushroom and onion mixture in a bowl, then stir in the yogurt. Add a little freshly ground black pepper and mix together. Liquidize for a few seconds and spoon into a pâté dish or four ramekins.

Store this mushroom pâté in the refrigerator for up to five days, or in the deep freeze. Spread on crackers, hot toast, or as a filling in vol-au-vent cases.

PORK PÂTÉ

100 g (4 oz) breadcrumbs
350 g (12 oz) lean pork
100 g (4 oz) pig's liver
180 ml (6 fluid oz) water
1 dessertspoon red peppers, finely chopped
1 small clove of garlic
salt and pepper

Wash and trim the liver and pork of any gristle and fat, chop and place in a pressure cooker with the water, a little salt and pepper and the crushed clove of garlic. Cook for 15 minutes at 15 lb pressure. Allow to cool, then pass through a liquidizer. Mix in the red peppers, the breadcrumbs and a little more seasoning, if required. Pour into a straight-sided ovenware dish, cover with baking paper and tie down. Stand the dish in a tray of water and cook for 2 hours in a hot oven (Gas Mark 6, 400°F, 200°C).

Remove from the oven and cover with a plate. Leave to cool then store in the refrigerator.

SAVOURY BEEF ON TOAST

100 g (4 oz) cold roast beef, finely minced

25 g (1 oz) breadcrumbs

$1/_4$ teaspoon parsley, chopped

rind of $1/_2$ lemon, grated

1 tablespoon tomato sauce

1 tablespoon hot water

knob of butter

salt and pepper

Heat together all the ingredients in a saucepan, blending well with a fork. This is delicious spread on hot buttered toast or used as a sandwich filling and is an interesting way to use up the end of a joint.

SIMPLE PÂTÉ

100 g (4 oz) breadcrumbs
180 ml (6 fluid oz) water
225 g (8 oz) sausagemeat
225 g (8 oz) smoked bacon
1 teaspoon lemon juice
$^1/_2$ teaspoon garlic purée

Put the bacon and the water in a pressure cooker and cook for 10 minutes at 15 lb pressure. Allow to cool, remove any bones from the bacon and pass through a mincing machine or liquidizer. Add the sausagemeat, garlic and lemon juice, and mix well together in the stock in the pressure cooker before adding the breadcrumbs. Spoon into an ovenware dish, cover with baking paper and tie down. Stand the dish in a tray of water and cook for $1^1/_2$ hours in a hot oven (Gas Mark 6, 400°F, 200°C).

Remove the simple pâté from the oven and cover with a plate. Leave to cool, then store in the refrigerator.

TASTY TOAST TOPPING

50 g (2 oz) breadcrumbs
225 g (8 oz) tomatoes, peeled and chopped
1 tablespoon butter or margarine
1 teaspoon onion, finely chopped
1 teaspoon parsley, finely chopped
1 teaspoon lemon juice
pinch of oregano
salt and pepper

Heat in a saucepan all the ingredients except
the breadcrumbs. Cook for a few minutes
before stirring in the breadcrumbs. Turn to
a very low heat with the lid on the pan and
simmer gently for a few more minutes, stirring
occasionally to prevent sticking.

Serve spread on hot buttered toast topped
with rashers of well-grilled bacon.

VEGETARIAN DISHES

We plough the fields, and scatter
The good seed on the land,
But it is fed and watered
By God's almighty hand;
He sends the snow in winter,
The warmth to swell the grain,
The breezes and the sunshine,
And soft refreshing rain.

Matthias Claudius

BAKED BEANS

50 g (2 oz) breadcrumbs
1 medium tin baked beans
1 tomato, sliced
50 g (2 oz) grated cheese
salt and pepper

Heat the baked beans in a saucepan, stirring occasionally and seasoning to taste. Pour into a small ovenware dish then sprinkle over the cheese, a layer of breadcrumbs and finally the tomato slices.

Cook under a warm grill for about 5 minutes. Garnish with a sprig of watercress and serve with a jacket potato and green salad.

Serves 2

BAKED TOMATOES

50 g (2 oz) breadcrumbs
50 g (1 lb) tomatoes
50 g (2 oz) grated cheese
salt and pepper
butter or margarine

Scald and peel 450 g (1 lb) of good evenly-shaped tomatoes. Place them in a deep ovenware dish. Sprinkle with a little salt and pepper, the breadcrumbs and the grated cheese. Bake in a hot oven (Gas Mark 6, 400°F, 200°C) for 30 minutes. Before serving add a few pats of butter.

These baked tomatoes make a tasty starter or a good accompaniment to a main course.

Serves 2-4

CAULIFLOWER CHEESE

50 g (2 oz) breadcrumbs
100 g (4 oz) grated cheese
360 ml (12 fluid oz) milk
1 cauliflower
nutmeg, grated
salt and pepper
butter or margarine

Trim and wash a cauliflower and break into florets. Cook in salted water until tender. Pour the milk into a saucepan and bring to the boil. Turn off the heat, then add the breadcrumbs and beat well together with a wooden spoon. Add the butter, a pinch of salt, pepper and nutmeg, then add half the cheese and stir in well. Drain the cauliflower and place the florets in an ovenware dish, then pour over the sauce and sprinkle the remaining cheese on the top. Place under a hot grill for 10 minutes to brown.

This dish could be divided into individual dishes and served as a starter.

Serves 2-4

CHEDDAR CHEESE SNACK

50 g (2 oz) breadcrumbs
100 g (4 oz) mature cheddar cheese
450 g (1 lb) potatoes, peeled and cubed
25 g (1 oz) chives, finely chopped
black pepper
salt

For the sauce
600 ml (1 pint) milk
2 dessertspoons flour
12 g (¹/₂ oz) butter or margarine
pinch salt

Boil the potatoes in salted water for 5 minutes. Meanwhile make a white sauce as follows: mix the flour, salt and a little of the milk to a smooth paste. Bring to the boil the remainder of the milk in a saucepan. Add the paste and the butter or margarine and stir constantly until the sauce thickens.

Strain the potatoes and place in an oven-ware dish. Cut the cheese into rough-sized chunks and add to the potatoes. Sprinkle over the chives and a generous amount of freshly ground black pepper. Finally, pour over the white sauce and top with the breadcrumbs.

Cook in a moderate oven (Gas Mark 4, 350°F, 180°C) until the breadcrumbs are golden brown.

Serves 4

CHEESE AND ONION FLAN

50 g (2 oz) breadcrumbs

50 g (2 oz) grated cheese

1 small onion

butter or margarine

1 tablespoon top of the milk or cream

225 g (8 oz) shortcrust pastry

Grease and line a sandwich cake tin with shortcrust pastry. Chop the onion and mix it with the cheese and breadcrumbs. Put this mixture into the pastry case, pour the cream over it, and top with pats of butter or margarine.

Roll out any remaining pastry, cut it into strips and lay it on top of the flan to form a trellis or criss-cross pattern. Brush a little milk over it to glaze. Bake for 40 minutes in a moderate oven (Gas Mark 4, 350°F, 180°C).

Serves 4

Cheese and Onion Pie

50 g (2 oz) breadcrumbs
50 g (2 oz) grated cheese
1 small onion, grated
2 eggs
200 ml (1/3 pint) milk
salt and pepper
a little nutmeg, grated
225 g (8 oz) shortcrust pastry

Beat together the egg and milk and add to this the breadcrumbs, cheese and onion, salt and pepper to taste, and nutmeg. Pour into a well-greased pie dish and cover with pastry. Bake in a moderate oven (Gas Mark 4, 350°F, 180°C) for 40 minutes.

Serves 4

CHEESE AND POTATO PIE

50 g (2 oz) breadcrumbs

100 g (4 oz) grated cheese

4 medium potatoes

salt and pepper

a little nutmeg, grated

For the sauce

600 ml (1 pint) milk

2 dessertspoons flour

12 g (½ oz) butter or margarine

pinch salt

Grease well a casserole dish. Place a layer of thinly-sliced potatoes in the bottom. Cover with a sprinkling of cheese, salt, pepper and nutmeg. Continue in layers until all are used.

Make a white sauce as follows: mix the flour, salt and a little of the milk to a smooth paste. Bring to the boil the rest of the milk in a saucepan. Add the paste and the fat and stir constantly until the sauce thickens.

Pour the white sauce over the layers of potato and cheese and sprinkle the breadcrumbs on top. Cook with a lid on the dish for about 20 minutes. Remove the lid and cook for a further 10 minutes on the top shelf of the oven to brown.

Serves 2-4

CHEESE AND TOMATO CRÊPES

50 g (2 oz) breadcrumbs

50 g (2 oz) grated cheese

nutmeg

1 tablespoon milk

1 x 400 g (14 oz) tin tomatoes

1 small onion

1 dessertspoon vegetable oil

salt and pepper

For the pancakes

100 g (4 oz) self raising flour

200 ml ($^1/_3$ pint) milk

1 egg, beaten

1 tablespoon cooking oil

Make the pancakes as follows: mix together the flour and milk until well blended. Beat in the egg allowing air into the mixture. Pour a little of the cooking oil into a frying pan and heat. Divide the pancake mixture into four and pour in one quarter. Cook quickly on one side before turning or tossing to cook the other side. Repeat to make four pancakes and put them to one side.

Mix together the breadcrumbs, cheese and a small grating of nutmeg. Add the milk and bind together.

Spread the mixture onto the open pancakes, roll them up and place in a gratin dish. Finely chop the onion and fry in a little vegetable oil. Add the tomatoes and heat until boiling. Pour over the pancakes, adding a sprinkling of salt and pepper.

Cook in a hot oven (Gas Mark 6, 400°F, 200°C) for 15 minutes and serve while still hot.

Serves 4

CHEESE FRITTERS

50 g (2 oz) breadcrumbs
100 g (4 oz) grated cheese
1 egg
50 g (2 oz) margarine or cooking oil
salt and pepper

Beat the egg, then add to the other ingredients in a mixing bowl. Mix well together.

Pour some cooking oil or melt some margarine in a frying pan. When hot, drop the mixture from a tablespoon into it. Fry until golden brown. Drain well and serve hot.

Serves 2

CHEESE PUDDING

50 g (2 oz) breadcrumbs
100 g (4 oz) mature cheese, grated
1 tablespoon flour
1 egg, separated
25 g (1 oz) butter or margarine
300 ml ($^1/_2$ pint) milk
salt and pepper
a pinch of nutmeg, grated

Put the milk in a saucepan and bring to the boil. Remove from the heat and add the breadcrumbs, cheese, butter or margarine and flour. Leave to cool.

Beat the egg yolk and fold into the mixture in the saucepan. Whisk the egg white until it is stiff and frothy and fold in last of all. Pour into a 2-pint ovenware dish and bake for 20 minutes in a moderate oven (Gas Mark 4, 350°F, 180°C) until golden brown.

Serves 2

CHEESE SOUFFLÉ

100 g (4 oz) breadcrumbs
200 ml (¹/₃ pint) milk
100 g (4 oz) mature cheese, grated
1 tablespoon butter or margarine
3 eggs, separated
salt and pepper
a little nutmeg, grated

Mix together the milk, breadcrumbs, cheese and melted butter or margarine and add salt and pepper to taste. Beat well the yolks of the eggs and add to the mixture. Whisk the egg whites until stiff and fold in. Spoon into a greased soufflé dish and bake for 45 minutes in a hot oven (Gas Mark 6, 400°F, 200°C).

Serves 3-4

CORN-STUFFED PEPPERS

4 red peppers
50 g (2 oz) breadcrumbs
100 g (4 oz) sweetcorn
1 dessertspoon onion, finely chopped
1 dessertspoon parsley, finely chopped
1 dessertspoon tomato sauce
salt
a pinch of cayenne pepper
butter or margarine
watercress

Slice the top off each pepper and remove all the seeds and partitions. Cook in boiling water for 5 minutes and drain well.

To make the stuffing, mix together all but a sprinkling of the breadcrumbs, the sweetcorn, onion, parsley and tomato sauce. Add the seasoning to taste and a few drops of water to bind the mixture together.

Fill the peppers with the stuffing, sprinkling the tops with the remaining breadcrumbs. Top with a pat of butter. Stand them in a shallow greased ovenware dish filled with water. Bake for 35 minutes in a moderate oven (Gas Mark 4, 350°F, 180°C). Serve garnished with sprigs of watercress.

Serves 4

EGG AND CHEESE SNACK

50 g (2 oz) breadcrumbs
50 g (2 oz) mature cheese, grated
2 eggs and enough milk to make 200 ml (8 fluid oz)
salt and pepper
nutmeg, grated

Beat together in a mixing bowl the eggs, milk, a pinch of salt, pepper and nutmeg. Add the breadcrumbs and grated cheese and stir in well. Pour into a well-buttered ovenware dish and cook for 40 minutes in a moderate oven (Gas Mark 4, 350°F, 180°C).

Serves 2

EGG AND TOMATO DISH

100 g (4 oz) breadcrumbs

4 large tomatoes, peeled and sliced

225 g (8 oz) cooked potatoes, mashed

4 eggs

butter or margarine

salt and pepper

Grease an ovenware dish and sprinkle into the base nearly all the breadcrumbs. Place on top the sliced tomatoes and season. Add a layer of mashed potatoes and season again. Break the eggs on top of the potatoes and top with the remaining breadcrumbs. Add a few pats of butter or margarine and bake in a moderate oven (Gas Mark 4, 350°F, 180°C) for 25 minutes.

Serves 4

EGGS AU GRATIN

50 g (2 oz) breadcrumbs
100 g (4 oz) grated cheese
400 ml ($^2/_3$ pint) milk
1 tablespoon flour
$^1/_4$ teaspoon salt
$^1/_4$ teaspoon cayenne pepper
4 eggs, hard boiled
75 g (3 oz) butter or margarine

Melt the butter or margarine in a saucepan. Stir in the flour, then the milk and a little salt and pepper. Stir continuously until boiling and remove from the heat. Mix in half of the cheese to make a cheese sauce. Slice the hard boiled eggs and place evenly in an ovenware dish. Pour over the sauce, sprinkle with the breadcrumbs and the remaining cheese. Bake in a moderate oven (Gas Mark 4, 350°F, 180°C) for 30 minutes.

Serves 4

GENOESE EGGS

50 g (2 oz) breadcrumbs
4 eggs
175 g (6 oz) grated cheese
butter or margarine
salt and pepper
a little chopped parsley

Grease an ovenware dish and sprinkle in the grated cheese, reserving a little for the topping. Break in the eggs, add salt and pepper to taste and cover with breadcrumbs, a little grated cheese, and top with pats of butter or margarine. Bake for 15 minutes in a hot oven (Gas Mark 6, 400°F, 200°C). Serve hot, sprinkled with a little chopped parsley to garnish.

Serves 4

ONION PIE

175 g (6 oz) breadcrumbs
2 large onions, finely chopped
50 g (2 oz) butter or margarine
400 ml (²/₃ pint) milk
salt and pepper

Generously grease a pie dish and line with breadcrumbs. Fill with a layer of onions, salt and pepper to taste, pats of butter and a further layer of breadcrumbs. Continue in layers until all the ingredients are used, finishing with a layer of breadcrumbs. Pour the milk over the top and cook in a hot oven (Gas Mark 6, 400°F, 200°C) for 1 hour, when the top should be golden brown.

Serves 2

SPAGHETTI AND TOMATO CHEESE

50 g (2 oz) breadcrumbs

175 g (6 oz) broken spaghetti

50 g (2 oz) mature cheese, grated

1 x 400 g (14 oz) tin peeled tomatoes

1 egg, beaten

pinch of oregano

garlic clove, crushed

black pepper

salt

paprika

Cook the spaghetti in some salted water until tender and strain well. Place in a shallow ovenware dish. Mix together half the cheese, the beaten egg and the garlic and stir into the spaghetti. Chop the tomatoes and pour over the mixture, seasoning with some black pepper, paprika and the oregano. Mix together the breadcrumbs and the remaining cheese and sprinkle over the top. Cook in a hot oven (Gas Mark 6, 400°F, 200°C) until golden brown.

Serves 2

STUFFED ONIONS

50 g (2 oz) breadcrumbs
4 large onions
2 tablespoons cooked ham, chopped
1/2 teaspoon mustard
1 egg, beaten
butter or margarine

Skin the onions and boil them for 15 minutes in salted water. Drain well. Melt the butter or margarine in a saucepan and add the chopped ham, breadcrumbs and mustard. Mix well together and bind with the beaten egg.

Stand the onions in a buttered baking dish, cut a cross on the top of each one and form a hollow. Fill with the prepared mixture. Cover with greased paper and bake in a hot oven (Gas Mark 6, 400°F, 200°C) for 20 minutes.

Serves 2-4

FISH

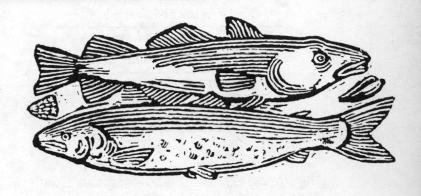

He only is the maker
Of all things near and far;
He paints the wayside flower;
He lights the evening star;
The winds and waves obey him,
By him the birds are fed;
Much more to us, his children,
He gives our daily bread.

Matthias Claudius

BAKED TROUT

4 small trout
100 g (4 oz) breadcrumbs
1 tablespoon soft margarine
1 tablespoon chives, chopped
1 teaspoon lemon juice
1 small onion, sliced
4 tomatoes, sliced
salt
black pepper

Wash and clean the trout. Leave to soak in salted water for a few minutes and wipe dry.

Mix together the margarine with the chives, lemon juice and a little black pepper. Spread this mixture over and inside the trout. Place on a shallow ovenware dish and sprinkle over the breadcrumbs. Garnish with onion rings and the sliced tomatoes. Sprinkle with a little salt and black pepper. Bake in a hot oven (Gas Mark 6, 400°F, 200°C) for 30 minutes.

Serve with new potatoes and parsley sauce.

Serves 4

COD AU GRATIN

50 g (2 oz) breadcrumbs
50 g (2 oz) mature cheese, grated
450 g (1 lb) boiled cod
butter or margarine
cayenne pepper
salt

For the sauce
600 ml (1 pint milk)
2 dessertspoons flour
50 g (2 oz) butter or margarine
salt

Make a white sauce as follows: mix the flour, salt and a little of the milk to a smooth paste. Bring to the boil the remainder of the milk in a saucepan. Add the paste and the butter or margarine and stir constantly until the sauce thickens.

Skin and bone the fish very carefully when cool and separate the flakes. Grease a flat ovenware dish. Put in alternate layers of fish, sauce and cheese, and season to taste (cayenne is hot!). Sprinkle on top the breadcrumbs and top with pats of butter. Heat through in a moderate oven (Gas Mark 4, 350°F, 180°C) for about 20 minutes.

Garnish with parsley and serve with mashed potatoes and a green vegetable.

Serves 3

FILLET OF PLAICE
WITH TOMATO

50 g (2 oz) breadcrumbs

2 fillets of plaice

2 tomatoes, peeled and sliced

lemon juice

salt and pepper

butter or margarine

Grease a pie dish and lay the fillets on the base. Sprinkle with lemon juice, salt and pepper, and cover with slices of peeled tomatoes. Season again to taste. Top with the breadcrumbs and pats of butter. Bake in a moderate oven (Gas Mark 4, 350°F, 180°C) for 30 minutes.

Serves 2

FILLETED MACKEREL

50 g (2 oz) breadcrumbs
1 egg
1 large mackerel
salt and pepper
1 level tablespoon cooking oil

Wash the fish in salted water, cut off the head and cut the fish from the bone on both sides. Cut each slice in two. Season well with salt and pepper. Beat the egg, dip each piece of fish into it, then cover with the breadcrumbs. Heat the oil in a frying pan and fry the fillets gently for 8 minutes on each side.

Serves 2-4

FISH AND TOMATO, STEAMED

350 g (12 oz) white fish, cooked

50 g (2 oz) breadcrumbs

4 large tomatoes

1 egg, beaten

25 g (1 oz) melted butter

Carefully remove all the skin and bones from the cold cooked fish and break up into pieces.

Remove the skin from the tomatoes by soaking for a few minutes in boiling water. Pass the tomatoes through a sieve to remove the seeds, if desired, then blend them in with the fish, breadcrumbs, melted butter and a well-beaten egg. Season to taste.

Check that four ovenware cups fit your steamer, then press the fish mixture into them, greasing beforehand. Cover with buttered paper and steam for 30 minutes.

Turn the cups onto a bed of curried rice. They will hold their shape and make a tasty and attractive supper dish.

Serves 4

FISH CAKES

225 g (8 oz) white fish, cooked

450 g (1 lb) potatoes, cooked and mashed

2 tablespoons butter or margarine

1 teaspoon parsley, chopped

1 egg, beaten

salt and pepper

50 g (2 oz) breadcrumbs

2 tablespoons cooking oil

Break up the cooked fish into flakes, removing all skin and bones. Melt the butter or margarine, add the parsley, fish and mashed potato, and season to taste. Mix well together.

Turn out onto a lightly floured board and form into rounds. Dip each round first into the egg, then into the breadcrumbs so that it is completely coated. Fry in hot oil on both sides until golden brown. This recipe makes eight good-sized fish cakes.

Serves 4-8

FISH CROQUETTES

175 g (6 oz) breadcrumbs
175 g (6 oz) white fish, flaked
1 teaspoon parsley, chopped
1 egg, beaten
salt and pepper
mixed herbs

Mix together the breadcrumbs with the fish, parsley, a pinch of mixed herbs, salt and pepper to taste. Bind all together with the well-beaten egg. Form into rounds with floured hands.

Place the croquettes in the basket of a chip pan and pour enough oil into the pan to cover and deep fry. Heat the oil until bubbling, then fry the fish croquettes until golden. Drain well on kitchen paper before serving.

Serves 4

FISH FOR TWO

50 g (2 oz) breadcrumbs
2 pieces fish, fresh or frozen
400 ml (²/₃ pint) top of the milk, warmed
1 teaspoon parsley, chopped
butter or margarine
salt
black pepper

Grease an ovenware dish and put in the breadcrumbs, sprinkle with salt and pepper and pour over the warm milk. Place the fish on top, sprinkle with parsley, and season to taste. Dot with butter or margarine and cook in a moderate to low oven (Gas Mark 3, 325°F, 170°C) for 30 minutes.

Serves 2

FISH PASTIES

2 pieces white fish
25 g (1 oz) breadcrumbs
1 hard-boiled egg, chopped
25 g (1 oz) butter or margarine, melted
1 teaspoon chives, chopped
100 g (4 oz) puff pastry
salt and pepper

Poach the fish in a little milk or water until cooked. When cool, remove any skin and bones from the fish and mix with the breadcrumbs, chopped egg and chives, and season to taste. Pour in the melted butter and mix well together.

Roll out the puff pastry very thinly and cut into squares about two inches by two inches. Place a little of the fish mixture on each square, brush some milk on the edges, then fold like an envelope. Use a fork to seal the edges, then brush the tops with milk. Bake in a hot oven (Gas Mark 7, 425°F, 220°C) for about 25 minutes, until golden.

Serves 2

Fish Pudding

225 g (8 oz) white fish, poached
50 g (2 oz) breadcrumbs
200 ml (⅓ pint) milk, warmed
1 egg, beaten
1 dessertspoon tomato sauce
salt
cayenne pepper
butter or margarine

Place the breadcrumbs in a mixing bowl and pour over the warmed milk. Leave to cool.

Beat the breadcrumb mixture for a few minutes to make smooth and add to this the beaten egg. Mix well, and add the tomato sauce, salt and a pinch of cayenne pepper, and lastly the fish. Place in a well-greased ovenware dish and top with pats of butter or margarine. Bake in a moderate oven (Gas Mark 4, 350°F, 180°C) for 30 minutes.

Serves 2

LOBSTER FLAN

50 g (2 oz) breadcrumbs

1 teaspoon lemon juice

1 x 200 g (7 oz) tin lobster

salt and pepper

175 g (6 oz) puff pastry

For the sauce

300 ml (¹/₂ pint) milk

1 dessertspoon flour

6 g (¹/₄ oz) butter or margarine

salt

Make half a pint of white sauce as follows: mix the flour, salt and a little of the milk to a smooth paste. Bring to the boil the remainder of the milk in a saucepan. Add the paste and the butter or margarine and stir constantly until the sauce thickens.

Grease and line a flan dish with the puff pastry. Bone the lobster and cut it up into small pieces. Mix the lobster with the lemon juice, white sauce, salt and pepper to taste. Pour into the flan case, top with breadcrumbs and pats of butter. Bake in a moderate oven (Gas Mark 4, 350°F, 180°C) for 30 minutes.

Serves 2-4

MACKEREL WITH GOOSEBERRIES

50 g (2 oz) breadcrumbs
100 g (4 oz) gooseberries
200 ml ($^1/_3$ pint) water
100 g (4 oz) sugar
juice and finely grated rind of 1 lemon
2 mackerel
salt and pepper
butter or margarine

Place the gooseberries in a shallow ovenware dish. Sprinkle the sugar over the gooseberries, then pour in the water.

Clean and guy the mackerel leaving on the head and tail. Place the fish on top of the gooseberries and pour over it the lemon juice with the rind. Season to taste and add a generous knob of butter or margarine. Sprinkle over the breadcrumbs. Cook in a hot oven (Gas Mark 6, 400°F, 200°C) for 45 minutes.

Serves 2

SALMON AND PRAWN CRÊPES

1 small tin red salmon

50 g (2 oz) breadcrumbs

1 small jar salmon spread

butter or margarine

1 dessertspoon lemon juice

1 teaspoon parsley, chopped

50 g (2 oz) prawns

black pepper

For the pancakes

100 g (4 oz) self raising flour

200 ml (1/3 pint) milk

1 egg, beaten

1 tablespoon cooking oil

For the sauce

600 ml (1 pint) milk

2 dessertspoons flour

12 g (1/2 oz) butter or margarine

salt

Make the pancakes as follows: mix together
the flour and milk until well blended. Beat in

the egg allowing air into the mixture. Pour a little of the cooking oil into a frying pan and heat. Divide the pancake mixture into four and pour in one quarter. Cook quickly on one side before turning or tossing to cook the other side. Repeat to make four pancakes and put them to one side.

Take the salmon and juices, remove the bones and mix together with the lemon juice, black pepper and breadcrumbs. Spread each of the four pancakes with a quarter of the mixture, roll up and place in a gratin dish, scattering around them a few prawns.

Make the white sauce as follows: melt the butter or margarine in a saucepan and add two dessertspoons of flour and one pint of milk. Bring to the boil, stirring constantly with a wooden spatula. When thickened, remove from the heat and spoon in the salmon spread. Mix well and pour over the pancakes. Sprinkle with black pepper and parsley. Cook in a medium hot oven (Gas Mark 5, 375°F, 190°C) for 15 minutes.

Serves 4

SALMON CROQUETTES

175 g (6 oz) breadcrumbs

175 g (6 oz) cooked salmon

25 g (1 oz) flour

butter or margarine

1 teaspoon parsley, chopped

nutmeg, grated

juice of ½ lemon

1 egg, separated

cooking oil

salt and pepper

For the sauce

200 ml (⅓ pint) milk

1 dessertspoon cornflour

knob of butter or margarine

Make a thick white sauce by heating the milk in a saucepan, melting in it the butter or margarine and stirring in the cornflour with a wooden spoon until it thickens. Grate into the sauce a little nutmeg. Add the parsley, fish and breadcrumbs, seasoning to taste. Heat through, then whisk into it the egg yolk that has been beaten with the lemon juice. Leave to cool.

When cold, divide into tablespoons, dip into flour and brush over with the beaten egg white. Cover with breadcrumbs. Fry in hot oil until golden.

Serves 3

SARDINE PANCAKES

50 g (2 oz) breadcrumbs
1 small tin sardines in oil
3 medium potatoes
1 teaspoon lemon juice
vegetable oil

Peel the potatoes and boil in salted water. Mash well.

Place the sardines and the oil in a mixing bowl with the lemon juice and mix together with a fork. Mix in the breadcrumbs, then the mashed potatoes. Shape into rounds and fry in vegetable oil until golden brown. Serve hot with parsley sauce.

Serves 3

SARDINE ROLL

---

50 g (2 oz) breadcrumbs

---

1 tin sardines in oil

---

juice and finely grated rind of ¹/₂ lemon

---

175 g (6 oz) puff pastry

Mix together the sardines with the oil and the breadcrumbs. Add the lemon rind to the mixture with the strained lemon juice and mix well together.

Roll out an oblong shape of puff pastry. Spread onto it the prepared mixture, then roll it up. Brush some milk on the edges to seal, and on the outside to glaze. Cook on a greased baking tray for 25 minutes in a hot oven (Gas Mark 6, 400°F, 200°C). This sardine roll is delicious served hot with parsley sauce and boiled potatoes.

For buffet suppers, try slicing the roll into half-inch pieces before placing in the oven. Cook in the same way for 20 minutes and leave to cool before serving.

Serves 3-4

SARDINES AND CHEESE

25 g (1 oz) breadcrumbs
1 tin sardines in oil
juice of ½ lemon
50 g (2 oz) grated cheese
1 egg yolk
salt and pepper

Warm the sardines in a pan with the oil and lemon juice. Pick them out and lay on a hot dish, sprinkling with grated cheese. Pour the breadcrumbs into the pan containing the oil and lemon juice and beat in the egg yolk. Spoon on top of the sardines and place under the grill for a few minutes to brown.

Serves 2

Smoked Haddock in Parsley Sauce

50 g (2 oz) breadcrumbs

2 pieces smoked haddock

butter or margarine

salt and pepper

For the sauce

600 ml (1 pint) milk

1 dessertspoon flour

knob of butter or margarine

pinch salt

2 dessertspoons parsley, finely chopped

Make a thin parsley sauce as follows: mix a dessertspoon of flour in a basin with a little of the milk, and a pinch of salt. Pour the remainder of the milk into a pan with a knob of butter and bring to the boil. Add to this the flour mixture, stirring all the time. Finally, add the chopped parsley.

Boil the haddock in water for 10 minutes. Grease an ovenware dish and line the base with breadcrumbs. Sprinkle with salt and pepper. Strain the fish and place on top of the breadcrumbs. Pour over the parsley sauce. Cook in a low oven (Gas Mark 2, 300°F, 150°C) for 30 minutes.

Serves 2

SOLE AU GRATIN

75 g (3 oz) brown breadcrumbs
1 small onion, finely chopped
1 teaspoon parsley, finely chopped
100 g (4 oz) button mushrooms, chopped
1 tablespoon tomato purée
210 ml (7 fluid oz) water
salt and pepper
butter or margarine
2 pieces lemon sole

Generously grease a gratin dish and spread in the base the very finely chopped onion. Add some of the parsley, a few chopped mushrooms, and half the breadcrumbs.

Clean, skin and trim the fish and lay them on the breadcrumb base. Sprinkle with a little more parsley, salt and pepper to taste. Top with breadcrumbs, some pats of butter, and the remaining mushrooms. Mix the tomato purée in the water and pour over. Bake for 25 minutes in a moderate oven (Gas Mark 5, 375°F, 190°C). This makes a delicious meal for a special occasion and can be served from the gratin dish.

For a more economical meal, use plaice and follow these instructions.

Serves 2

TASTY COD SUPPER

50 g (2 oz) breadcrumbs
2 cod steaks
1 tablespoon suet, chopped
1 egg, beaten
1 tablespoon parsley, chopped
1 lemon rind, finely grated
1/2 teaspoon mixed herbs
200 ml (1/3 pint) water
1 teaspoon yeast extract
salt and pepper

Mix together the breadcrumbs, suet, parsley, lemon rind and mixed herbs, adding salt and pepper to taste. Bind all together with the beaten egg and place in a well-greased ovenware dish. Place the cod steaks on top. Mix the yeast extract into the water and pour over the fish and breadcrumbs, adding a little more salt and pepper to the fish. Cook in a moderate oven (Gas Mark 4, 350°F, 180°C) for 1 hour.

Serves 2

TINNED PILCHARDS WITH SALAD

50 g (2 oz) breadcrumbs
¹/₄ teaspoon salt
1 tablespoon vinegar
1 tablespoon olive oil
1 tablespoon lemon juice
black pepper
1 small tin pilchards in tomato sauce

Mix the breadcrumbs with a little freshly ground black pepper and place in a non-metallic serving dish.

Whisk together the vinegar, salt and oil with a fork. Pour over the breadcrumbs. Place the pilchards on top of the mixture and pour over the tomato sauce, sprinkling with the lemon juice and a little black pepper. Cover the dish and leave overnight in the refrigerator to marinate.

Sprinkle the top with some finely chopped chives or spring onion and a little olive oil. Serve with a green salad.

Serves 3

Main Courses

We thank thee then, O Father,
For all things bright and good,
The seedtime and the harvest,
Our life, our health, our food.
No gifts have we to offer
For all thy love imparts,
But that which thou desirest,
Our humble, thankful hearts.

Matthias Claudius

A Simple Supper Dish

100 g (4 oz) cut macaroni
50 g (2 oz) breadcrumbs
100 g (4 oz) grated cheese
450 g (1 lb) tomatoes, skinned and chopped
butter or margarine
salt and pepper

Boil the macaroni in salted water until tender and drain well. Grease an ovenware dish and place into this alternate layers of macaroni, cheese, and tomatoes, seasoning each layer. Cover with breadcrumbs and top with pats of butter and a little extra cheese. Cook for 30 minutes on the top shelf of a hot oven (Gas Mark 6, 400°F, 200°C) until golden brown.

Serves 2

A Tasty Snack

50 g (2 oz) breadcrumbs
2 tomatoes, skinned and sliced
1 rasher of bacon, cut small
50 g (2 oz) grated cheese
salt and pepper
100 g (4 oz) shortcrust pastry

Line two heat-proof saucers with shortcrust pastry. Cover with some slices of seasoned tomato, sprinkle over the breadcrumbs, then the cheese, and decorate with a slice of tomato. Sprinkle with a little more salt and pepper and top with small pieces of bacon. Cook for 20 minutes in a moderate oven (Gas Mark 5, 375°F, 190°C).

Serves 2

Useful hint
To remove the odour when boiling cabbage, place a dessertspoon of breadcrumbs into the pan when the water starts to boil. The smell will vanish immediately.

BACON AND CABBAGE DISH

50 g (2 oz) breadcrumbs
50 g (2 oz) grated cheese
1 onion, roughly chopped
1 carrot, roughly chopped
450 g (1 lb) white cabbage
300 ml ($\frac{1}{2}$ pint) water
1 stock cube
1 tablespoon cooking oil
225 g (8 oz) streaky bacon

Wash the cabbage and chop into chunky pieces, leaving in a colander to drain. Heat the oil in a frying pan (with a lid) and add the chopped onion and carrot. Fry for 5 minutes. Add the cabbage and a sprinkling of salt and pepper. Fry this also for 5 minutes. Dissolve the stock cube in half a pint of water, add to the vegetables and bring to the boil. Lower the heat, place the lid tightly on the pan and simmer for 25 minutes.

Pour the vegetables into an ovenware dish and cover with a mixture of breadcrumbs and cheese. Add a sprinkling of freshly ground black pepper and top with rashers of streaky bacon. Cook on the middle shelf of a hot oven (Gas Mark 6, 400°F, 200°C) until golden brown.

Serves 4

BACON AND TOMATOES

50 g (2 oz) breadcrumbs
450 g (1 lb) tomatoes, skinned and sliced
1 small onion, finely chopped
1 teaspoon parsley, chopped
1 teaspoon lemon juice
butter or margarine
salt and pepper
4 squares of fried bread
4 rashers of bacon

Place the sliced tomatoes in a saucepan with the butter or margarine, parsley, onion, lemon juice, breadcrumbs, salt, pepper and a very little water. Simmer for 10-15 minutes. Arrange the squares of well-drained fried bread on a hot dish and pour over the tomato mixture. Top with rashers of grilled bacon.

Serves 4

BEEF AND OREGANO

50 g (2 oz) breadcrumbs
450 g (1 lb) stewing steak, cubed
1 x 400 g (14 oz) tin peeled tomatoes
1 onion, chopped
1 carrot, diced
1 small green pepper, chopped
600 ml (1 pint) water
25 g (1 oz) butter or margarine
salt and pepper
oregano
paprika

Melt the butter in a frying pan and add the cubed beef. Fry for 10 minutes, then place in a casserole dish. Add the carrot, onion, a pinch of oregano, salt, pepper and paprika to taste. Pour over the water, and cook uncovered in a hot oven (Gas Mark 6, 400°F, 200°C) for 1 hour. Remove from the oven and add the de-seeded, chopped green pepper, the tomatoes and the breadcrumbs. Stir so that all the ingredients are well mixed, then return to the oven and cook for a further hour. Delicious served with potatoes and vegetables or with noodles.

Serves 4

BEEF CAKES

225 g (8 oz) cold roast beef

100 g (4 oz) bacon

50 g (2 oz) breadcrumbs

1 large egg, beaten

salt and pepper

1 tablespoon cooking oil

1 small onion, sliced into rings

3 tomatoes, halved

Mince the leftovers from a joint of roast beef. Mix in the breadcrumbs and bind together with a beaten egg. Add a very little salt and a generous sprinkling of pepper. Form into squares and fry in hot cooking oil. This recipe is a delicious way to use up the end of a roast. Serve topped with fried onion rings and tomatoes.

Serves 4

BEEF CASSEROLE

1 tablespoon beef dripping or vegetable oil
450 g (1 lb) braising steak
1 large carrot, sliced
4 potatoes, peeled and halved
600 ml (1 pint) water
1 teaspoon salt
pepper
50 g (2 oz) breadcrumbs
¼ teaspoon gravy browning

Melt the fat in a frying pan and add the pieces of steak. Fry for 5 minutes on each side before placing in a casserole dish. Next fry the onions and carrots for 5 minutes and add these to the meat.

Pour into the frying pan the water, salt and pepper, breadcrumbs and gravy browning. Bring to the boil, then pour over the meat in the casserole. Put the peeled, halved potatoes on top of the casserole and cook in a hot oven (Gas Mark 7, 425°F, 220°C) for at least 1 hour. Serve with extra vegetables.

Serves 4

BEEF PUDDING

225 g (8 oz) minced beef

1 medium onion, chopped

1 small carrot, chopped

50 g (2 oz) green pepper, diced

50 g (2 oz) breadcrumbs

1 egg, beaten

$1/2$ beef stock cube

1 tablespoon boiling water

salt and pepper

For the suet crust pastry

175 g (6 oz) flour

75 g (3 oz) suet

$1/4$ teaspoon salt

90 ml (3 fluid oz) water

Place the minced beef, onion, carrot, green pepper and breadcrumbs into a mixing bowl,

and mix well together with the beaten egg. Put half a beef stock cube into a basin, add the boiling water and stir until dissolved. Then add to the mixture with a pinch of salt and pepper, mixing well together.

Line a pudding basin with the suet crust pastry, leaving enough over the edge of the basin to cover the mixture. Seal with a little water. Cover with greaseproof paper and tie down. Stand the basin in a pan of boiling water which reaches half-way up the side. Simmer for $1\frac{1}{2}$ hours, checking the water level occasionally.

Serve hot with some extra gravy, boiled potatoes and vegetables. When cold it can be sliced and served with a salad or chipped potatoes. A filling and versatile meal!

Serves 4

BRAISING STEAK AND MUSHROOMS

700 g (1 ¹/₂ lb) braising steak, cut thinly
50 g (2 oz) breadcrumbs
1 tablespoon tomato sauce
600 ml (1 pint) water
¹2 onion, chopped finely
100 g (4 oz) mushrooms
salt and pepper

Wash and dry the mushrooms and remove the stems. Divide the steak into three portions. Chop up the mushroom stems and onion and spread onto each piece of steak. Sprinkle on top some breadcrumbs, add a little seasoning, then roll up the meat and tie with white cotton.

Place the rolled steaks in a pan, add the water, mushroom tops, tomato sauce and a little more seasoning. Bring to the boil then turn the heat very low, put the lid on tightly and simmer gently for 1 hour. Remove the lid, add a tablespoon of breadcrumbs and continue cooking for a further hour, by which time the meat should be tender. Remove the cotton and place in a serving dish surrounded with mushrooms.

Serves 3

CANNELON

175 g (6 oz) breadcrumbs
450 g (1 lb) cooked beef
225 g (8 oz) cooked ham
2 eggs, beaten
salt and pepper
parsley, chopped
2 tablespoons water

Mince finely the beef and the ham, add the breadcrumbs, salt, pepper and parsley and mix well together. Add the beaten eggs and the water and form into a roll. Tie up in a floured pudding cloth and steam for 2 hours.

Serve hot with gravy or chilled, dressed with salad.

Serves 4-6

Useful hint
For thickening gravy, put some breadcrumbs into a warm oven to dry and crisp. Place on a piece of clean kitchen paper and roll with a rolling pin until fine. Store in an airtight container until required. Pour water into your frying pan and bring to the boil before adding breadcrumbs.

Chicken and Bacon Mould

50 g (2 oz) breadcrumbs
1 ¹/₂ kg (3 lb) chicken
100 g (4 oz) streaky bacon
200 ml (¹/₃ pint) water
1 hard-boiled egg, sliced

Place the fresh or well-defrosted chicken in a pressure cooker with the giblets and the bacon. Add ¹/₃ pint of water and a little pepper. Cook at 15 lb pressure for about 1 hour, until the meat falls off the bones.

Remove the meat and bones from the pressure cooker and add the breadcrumbs to the stock. Bring to the boil, then turn the heat to very low and simmer for a few minutes. Turn off the heat and leave to cool slowly.

Mince the skin from the chicken with the giblets and the bacon, then add these to the stock and breadcrumbs in the pan. Remove all the bones from the chicken and place the chicken meat in the stock. Stir all the ingredients in the pan together. Add a little more seasoning at this stage if required.

Spoon the mixture into a mould, adding the sliced hard boiled egg when half filled. Pour in the remainder. Place in the refrigerator overnight to set. Delicious served with pickles or salad.

Serves 6

Chicken Casserole

1 ¹/₂ kg (3 lb) chicken
50 g (2 oz) breadcrumbs
1 onion, chopped
2 carrots, chopped
1 dessertspoon rice
1 dessertspoon dried peas
600 ml (1 pint) water
dripping or cooking oil
salt and pepper
1 teaspoon sage

Cut the chicken into joints with a sharp knife. Heat the oil or dripping in a frying pan and fry the chicken joints until golden. Remove from the fat and place in a casserole dish.

Fry the onion and carrot in the juices left in the pan, adding salt and pepper to taste and the dried sage. Next add the water and bring to the boil. Add the breadcrumbs, then pour this mixture over the chicken joints in the casserole. Finally add the rice and dried peas. Cook on a low shelf in a moderate oven (Gas Mark 4, 350°F, 180°C) for 1 hour. Add extra water as necessary.

Serves 6

CHICKEN SAUTÉ

4 chicken joints
50 g (2 oz) breadcrumbs
1 large onion, sliced into rings
50 g (2 oz) button mushrooms
600 ml (1 pint) water
25 g (1 oz) butter or margarine
2 tablespoons tomato purée
1/2 teaspoon mixed herbs
salt and pepper

Using a saucepan with a lid, sauté the chicken joints in the butter or margarine, tossing frequently to prevent burning. After a few minutes add the onion rings and continue to sauté until they are turning brown. Add the tomato purée, mushrooms, salt and pepper to taste. Pour in the water and add the breadcrumbs. Put the lid on the pan and simmer gently for 1 hour, stirring occasionally. Alternatively, place in a covered casserole dish and cook in a pre-heated moderate oven (Gas Mark 4, 350°F, 180°C) for 1 hour.

Serves 4

Corned Beef Savoury

1 x 350 g (12 oz) tin corned beef

50 g (2 oz) breadcrumbs

2 medium potatoes, boiled and mashed

1 tablespoon milk

butter or margarine

mustard

sweet chutney

Slice the corned beef and spread one slice with English mustard and the next with sweet chutney, sandwiching the two together. Continue to spread and sandwich until all the slices are used up in this way.

Grease a pie dish and spread in the mashed potatoes that have been softened with a little milk. Arrange the corned beef on the mashed potato, and top with the breadcrumbs and a few pats of butter. Bake in a moderate oven (Gas Mark 4, 350°F, 180°C) until warmed through with the topping well browned.

Serves 3-4

COTTAGE PIE

225 g (8 oz) minced beef
400 ml (²/₃ pint) water
50 g (2 oz) breadcrumbs
1 small onion, chopped
1 medium carrot, chopped
1 teaspoon vinegar
1 teaspoon gravy browning
salt and pepper
650 g (1¹/₂ lb) potatoes, peeled, boiled and mashed

Place the minced beef into a pan with the water and vinegar. Bring to the boil then simmer for about 10 minutes. Add the chopped carrots, onion, breadcrumbs, gravy browning and salt and pepper to taste. Continue to simmer for 30 minutes, stirring occasionally.

When cooked, pour into an ovenware dish. Spread the mashed potatoes on top and add a few pats of butter. Grill until the top is well browned.

Serves 2

CURRIED CHICKEN

75 g (3 oz) breadcrumbs
2 plump chicken legs
1 carrot, chopped
1 onion, chopped
600 ml (1 pint) water
1 tablespoon frozen peas
1 teaspoon curry paste
1/4 teaspoon garlic paste
salt and pepper

Roughly chop the carrot and the onion and place in the base of a casserole dish. Put on top the chicken legs and add the curry and garlic paste. Pour in the water, adding a little salt and pepper to taste. Top with the breadcrumbs. Cook in a hot oven (Gas Mark 6, 400°F, 200°C) until the curry is boiling. Lower the heat and continue to cook for 2 hours, uncovered. Add the peas for the last 30 minutes of the cooking time. Serve with potatoes and vegetables or boiled rice.

Serves 2

CURRIED RABBIT

50 g (2 oz) breadcrumbs
1 large onion, sliced into rings
butter or margarine
1 tablespoon curry powder
$\frac{1}{2}$ teaspoon garlic paste
1 teaspoon salt
pepper
1 jointed rabbit
600 ml (1 pint) water

Fry the onion rings in the butter or margarine, then lift them out and place in an oven casserole. Fry the rabbit pieces in the juices left in the pan for a few minutes on all sides. Add these to the onions in the casserole. Sprinkle into the frying pan the curry powder, garlic paste, salt and pepper, mixing well with the remaining juices. Pour in the water slowly, add the breadcrumbs and bring to the boil. Pour over the rabbit and onions.

Cook for 1 hour in a moderate oven (Gas Mark 4, 350°F, 180°C) until tender. Alternatively, cook in a pan on top of the cooker, stirring occasionally to prevent sticking. Serve with boiled rice.

Serves 4

FAGGOTS

225 g (8 oz) fresh pork slices
225 g (8 oz) lamb's liver
50 g (2 oz) breadcrumbs
1 onion, chopped
2 eggs, beaten
$1/_4$ teaspoon sage
$1/_4$ teaspoon thyme
salt and pepper
300 ml ($1/_2$ pint) water
1 beef stock cube

Mince together the pork, liver and onion. Add the thyme and sage, salt and pepper to taste. Mix in well. Place in a pudding basin, cover with greased paper and tie down. Steam for 1 hour.

Pour off any surplus fat and leave to go cold.

Mix in the breadcrumbs and two well-beaten eggs. With floured hands, form into rounds and place in a greased dish. Pour round some gravy made with a beef stock cube and bake for 25 minutes in a hot oven (Gas Mark 6, 400°F, 200°C).

Serves 4

GREEN PEPPERS, STUFFED

4 green peppers
50 g (2 oz) breadcrumbs
100 g (4 oz) cooked ham, chopped
1 dessertspoon onion, chopped
1 dessertspoon parsley, chopped
1 dessertspoon tomato sauce
salt and pepper
butter or margarine
200 ml ($^1/_3$ pint) water

Cut a slice off the top of each pepper and remove all the seeds and partitions. Cook in boiling water for 5 minutes and drain well.

Make some stuffing by mixing all but a few of the breadcrumbs, the finely chopped ham, onion, parsley and tomato sauce. Add the salt and pepper to taste and a few drops of water to bind the mixture all together.

Fill the peppers with the stuffing, sprinkling the tops with the remaining breadcrumbs. Top with a pat of butter. Stand them in a shallow greased ovenware dish and pour in the water. Bake for 35 minutes in a moderate oven (Gas Mark 4, 350°F, 180°C).

Serves 2-4

HAM AND CHEESE ROLLS

50 g (2 oz) breadcrumbs
100 g (4 oz) grated cheese
4 slices boiled ham
1 dessertspoon flour
300 ml (¹/₂ pint) milk
pepper
butter or margarine

Mix together the breadcrumbs with half the grated cheese. Add a little milk to bind together and place a quarter of the mixture on each slice of ham. Make it into rolls and place in an ovenware dish.

Put into a saucepan the milk, flour, a pat of butter and a little black pepper. Bring to the boil, stirring constantly. Remove from the heat and stir in the remainder of the grated cheese. Pour over the ham rolls in the dish and bake in a hot oven (Gas Mark 6, 400°F, 200°C) for 15 minutes, until the ham and cheese rolls are heated through.

Serves 4

HAM AND EGGS, BAKED

225 g (8 oz) frying ham
4 eggs
50 g (2 oz) breadcrumbs
1 tablespoon cooking oil
butter or margarine
salt and pepper

Cut up the frying ham into small pieces and fry lightly in hot cooking oil. Place in a greased dish. Break the eggs onto the ham so that they cover it completely. Sprinkle with salt and pepper, and cover with the breadcrumbs. Bake for 10 minutes in a moderate oven (Gas Mark 4, 350°F, 180°C) until the eggs are cooked.

Serves 4

HAM AND POTATO CAKES

4 medium potatoes, peeled, boiled and mashed

100 g (4 oz) cooked ham, chopped

1 tablespoon onion, chopped

1 egg, beaten

50 g (2 oz) breadcrumbs

2 tablespoons cooking oil

salt and pepper

Mince the ham finely and mix with the mashed potato, salt and pepper to taste. Brown the chopped onion in some hot oil and mix in with the ham and potato. Bind with a well-beaten egg. Drop a tablespoon of the mixture into the breadcrumbs and form into a round. Continue until all is used up. Fry the ham and potato cakes in hot oil until golden.

Serves 2-3

HAM BALLS

50 g (2 oz) breadcrumbs

50 g (2 oz) cooked ham, finely chopped

1 egg, beaten

2 tablespoons flour

pepper

cooking oil

Mix the beaten egg into the breadcrumbs and ham and add a little pepper to taste. Form into rounds with floured hands and fry in deep fat. Drain well on kitchen paper before serving.

Serves 2

Ham Cakes

50 g (2 oz) breadcrumbs
175 g (6 oz) cold boiled ham, minced
cayenne pepper
25 g (1 oz) butter or margarine
1 small onion, minced
cooking oil
a little water

Mix together the breadcrumbs, finely minced ham and onion. Melt the butter and pour into the mixture. Add a pinch of cayenne pepper and knead together. If too dry, a very little water may be added. Form into rounds half an inch thick and fry in hot fat until golden, draining well before serving.

Serves 2

HOT POT

450 g (1 lb) stewing steak
1 large onion, chopped
50 g (2 oz) breadcrumbs
1 kg (2 lb) old potatoes, peeled and thinly sliced
1 dessertspoon vinegar
1 teaspoon salt
pepper
600 ml (1 pint) water
1 beef stock cube

Cut the beef into small cubes and place it with the chopped onion in a pressure cooker. Add a pint of water and the vinegar and cook at 15 lb pressure for 30 minutes until tender.

Put a layer of sliced potato in an ovenware dish, pour over the meat and stock and sprinkle the beef stock cube over the top. Cover with another layer of potato and sprinkle with salt and pepper. Sprinkle the top with breadcrumbs and cook for 30 minutes on the bottom shelf of a hot oven (Gas Mark 6, 400°F, 200°C) until the potatoes are tender. Move to the top shelf to brown.

Serves 3

LAMB CASSEROLE

50 g (2 oz) breadcrumbs
1 medium onion, chopped
1 medium carrot, sliced
1 lean breast of lamb, chopped
1 tablespoon vegetable oil
600 ml (1 pint) water
$\frac{1}{2}$ teaspoon dried rosemary
$\frac{1}{2}$ teaspoon thyme
salt and pepper

Ask the butcher to chop the lean breast of lamb. Soak it for a few minutes in salted water to draw out any bone splinters, then dry in kitchen paper. Add the lamb to a frying pan with the cooking oil and cook gently until golden brown.

Remove the meat from the pan and place in a casserole dish. Add to the juices left in the pan the carrot and onion, salt and pepper to taste and the dried herbs. Fry for a few minutes before pouring away the fat. Add the breadcrumbs and water to the vegetables, bring to the boil, then pour over the meat in the casserole. Cook in a hot oven (Gas Mark 6, 400°F, 200°C) for $1\frac{1}{2}$ hours. Check during this time to see if more water is needed.

Serves 4

Lamb Chops with Thyme

50 g (2 oz) breadcrumbs
200 ml (¹/₃ pint) water
¹/₂ vegetable stock cube
salt and pepper
¹/₄ teaspoon dried thyme
2 lamb chops

Dissolve half a vegetable stock cube in ¹/₃ pint of hot water. Pour over the breadcrumbs in an ovenware dish. Place on top two thick-cut lamb chops and sprinkle with thyme, salt and pepper. Cook in a preheated hot oven (Gas Mark 7, 425°F, 220°C) for 45 minutes. Serve with boiled potatoes and garden peas.

Serves 2

LIVER AND LEEK CASSEROLE

50 g (2 oz) breadcrumbs
400 ml (²/₃ pint) water
450 g (1 lb) leeks, chopped
225 g (8 oz) lamb's liver
1 onion, sliced in rings
1 tablespoon vegetable oil
1 clove garlic, crushed
salt and pepper

Heat the oil in a frying pan, and add the onion rings, frying until golden brown. Place in a casserole dish.

Add the leeks to the remaining oil in the frying pan and season to taste. Fry until softened, then place on top of the onions.

Add the lamb's liver to the pan with extra oil if necessary. Fry, with the crushed clove of garlic, for a few minutes on each side, then place on top of the leeks.

Pour the water into the frying pan and bring to the boil with the juices. Pour over the liver, and add more seasoning to taste. Sprinkle over the breadcrumbs and cook for 30 minutes in a hot oven (Gas Mark 6, 400°F, 200°C). Serve with potatoes and a green vegetable.

Serves 4

LIVER AND ONIONS

50 g (2 oz) breadcrumbs
1 onion, sliced into rings
600 ml (1 pint) water
225 g (8 oz) lamb's liver
225 g (8 oz) streaky bacon
1 tablespoon vegetable oil
salt and pepper

Slice the liver thinly and sauté in the hot oil to seal in the juices. Cut the rind off the bacon and roll each piece, tying with cotton to keep in place. Drain the liver and place in an ovenware dish. Fry the sliced onions in the remaining oil, adding a little extra if necessary. Place on top of the liver, sprinkle with breadcrumbs, top with rolls of bacon and add the water, salt and pepper to taste. Cook in a hot oven (Gas Mark 6, 400°F, 200°C) for 1 hour. Serve with boiled potatoes and vegetables.

Serves 4

MEAT LOAF

450 g (1 lb) minced beef
50 g (2 oz) breadcrumbs
1 egg, beaten
200 ml ($^1/_3$ pint) milk
1 carrot, grated
1 small pepper, minced
1 small onion, chopped finely
1 teaspoon salt
$^1/_2$ teaspoon pepper

Mix together all the ingredients, binding with the beaten egg. Fill a greased 1 lb loaf tin with the mixture and bake uncovered for 40 minutes in a moderate oven (Gas Mark 4, 350°F, 180°C). Turn out of the tin and serve surrounded with potatoes and vegetables.

Serves 4

MINCED MEAT CASSEROLE

450 g (1 lb) minced beef
600 ml (1 pint) water
1 teaspoon vinegar
50 g (2 oz) breadcrumbs
1 medium carrot, sliced
12 small shallots or 1 large onion
1 teaspoon salt
1 dessertspoon Worcestershire sauce
pepper
gravy browning

Put the lean minced beef into a pan with the water and vinegar and bring to the boil. Turn the heat to very low and simmer gently with the lid on the pan for 10 minutes. Add the breadcrumbs, carrots, onions, salt and pepper, Worcestershire sauce and gravy browning and return to boiling point. Pour into a casserole dish and finish cooking uncovered in a moderate oven (Gas Mark 4, 350°F, 180°C). Remove when the liquid has thickened and reduced and serve with boiled potatoes and green vegetables.

Serves 4

MUTTON CURRY

50 g (2 oz) breadcrumbs
450 g (1 lb) mutton, cubed
2 onions, chopped
25 g (1 oz) butter or margarine
1 dessertspoon curry powder
1 dessertspoon sweet chutney
1 apple, chopped
50 g (2 oz) sultanas
2 tablespoons desiccated coconut
salt and pepper
600 ml (1 pint) water

Melt the butter or margarine in a saucepan and add the onions and the cubed meat. Cook together for a few minutes before adding the peeled and chopped apple, chutney, curry powder, ginger and sultanas. Season to taste, stir well together and add the breadcrumbs. Pour in the water and bring to the boil. Turn the heat very low and simmer gently with the lid on the pan until the meat is tender. Garnish with desiccated coconut and serve with boiled rice. (This dish is equally good with lamb if mutton is not available.)

Serves 4

OPEN CHICKEN PIE

50 g (2 oz) breadcrumbs
200 ml (7 fluid oz) water
1½ kg (3 lb) chicken
salt and pepper
225 g (8 oz) shortcrust pastry

Cook a small chicken in a pressure cooker with the water and a pinch of salt and pepper. When the meat falls away from the bones, allow to cool then remove all the skin and bones. Leave in the refrigerator overnight to set.

Line a deep sandwich tin with 8 oz of shortcrust pastry. Fill with the chicken and the jelly and top with the breadcrumbs, adding a little salt and pepper. Bake in a moderate oven (Gas Mark 5, 375°F, 190°C) until golden. Delicious when served either hot or cold.

Serves 6

PASTA SURPRISE

50 g (2 oz) breadcrumbs

450 g (1 lb) tomatoes, peeled and chopped

1 large onion, chopped

225 g (8 oz) cut macaroni

225 g (8 oz) minced beef

1 dessertspoon cooking oil

25 g (1 oz) butter

1 teaspoon salt

¼ teaspoon pepper

Cook the macaroni in salted water, strain well and put to one side.

Heat the oil in a frying pan and add the minced beef. Cook for 10 minutes, stirring constantly to prevent sticking. Add the chopped onions and continue to cook until they are golden. Add the tomatoes, season generously and cook for a few more minutes. When the tomatoes are cooked, add the pasta and stir all the ingredients together. Pour into an ovenware dish, cover the top with breadcrumbs and add two or three pats of butter. Cook in a hot oven (Gas Mark 6, 400°F, 200°C) on the top shelf, until the crumbs are golden.

Serves 4

PORK CASSEROLE

50 g (2 oz) breadcrumbs
450 g (1 lb) lean pork steak, cut into chunks
600 ml (1 pint) water
1 onion, sliced into rings
1 carrot, sliced
1 cooking apple, peeled, cored and sliced
¹/₄ teaspoon garlic paste
¹/₂ teaspoon sage
salt and pepper

Remove any fat from the pork before cutting into chunks. Place in an ovenware dish and add to this all the other ingredients. Cook in a hot oven (Gas Mark 7, 425°F, 220°C) for 30 minutes, then lower the heat to Gas Mark 4, 350°F, 180°C, and cook gently for 1¹/₂ hours, or until the meat is tender. Remove the lid 20 minutes before the end of the cooking time to allow a little browning to occur. Serve with potatoes and vegetables.

Serves 4

PORK CHOPS WITH APPLE

50 g (2 oz) sage and onion stuffing (see Sauces and Stuffings section)
2 pork chops
1 cooking apple, peeled and cored
1 teaspoon sugar
1 dessertspoon vegetable oil
salt and pepper

Place the sage and onion stuffing in a basin and pour over enough boiling water to wet evenly.

Fry the chops in the hot oil for 3 minutes on each side to seal in the juices. Grease an ovenware dish and spread the stuffing onto the base. Add the pork chops and sprinkle with a little salt and pepper. Cut the apple into thick rings, arrange on top of the chops, and sprinkle with the sugar. Cook in a moderate oven (Gas Mark 4, 350°F, 180°C) for 30 minutes. Serve with boiled potatoes and vegetables.

Serves 2

Pork Chops with Orange Stuffing

50 g (2 oz) orange stuffing
(see Sauces and Stuffings section)

2 thick pork chops

1 dessertspoon cooking oil

2 tablespoons water

salt and pepper

Place the orange stuffing in the base of an ovenware dish. Trim some of the fat off the chops and fry in the oil for 10 minutes on each side. Place the chops onto the stuffing, adding a little salt and pepper to taste. Pour in the water and cook in a hot oven (Gas Mark 6, 400°F, 200°C) for 20 minutes with a lid on the dish. Remove the lid and cook for a further 20 minutes, checking to make sure it does not become over-dry. Serve with potatoes and vegetables.

Serves 2

PORK IN CREAMY SAUCE

100 g (4 oz) breadcrumbs
450 g (1 lb) pork steak
1 carrot, diced
1 onion, sliced into rings
2 bay leaves
400 ml ($^2/_3$ pint) water
2 tablespoons evaporated milk
salt and pepper

Trim all fat and any gristle off the pork, slice into thin pieces, then place in the pressure cooker. Add the carrot, onion, bay leaves and water and a little salt and pepper to taste. Cook for 30 minutes at 15 lb pressure until the meat is tender.

Remove the meat from the pressure cooker, place in a warm dish and keep warm. Remove the carrot, onion and bay leaves from the stock and pour the liquid through a sieve. Place the breadcrumbs and the stock in a saucepan and bring to the boil, stirring and beating with a wooden spoon until smooth. Remove from the heat and stir in the evaporated milk. Spread over the meat and serve with potatoes and vegetables.

Serves 4

PORK STEAK WITH LEEKS

50 g (2 oz) breadcrumbs
450 g (1 lb) pork steaks
1 onion, sliced into rings
1 carrot, chopped
1 leek, chopped
1 teaspoon sage
1 dessertspoon vegetable oil
salt and pepper
400 ml (²/₃ pint) water

Fry the pork steaks in the oil for 10 minutes each side then remove from the frying pan and put to one side. Add more oil if necessary and fry the onion rings with the chopped carrot until the onion is golden, seasoning to taste. Drain with a perforated spoon and place in the base of an ovenware dish.

Cook the chopped leeks in the remaining juices, adding the sage. Fry until transparent, then place on top of the fried carrot and onions in the dish. Top with the fried pork steaks.

Pour the water into the frying pan and bring to the boil, then pour over the meat and vegetables, adding a little extra salt and pepper to taste. Sprinkle the breadcrumbs over the top. Cook for 1 hour in a hot oven (Gas Mark 6, 400°F, 200°C).

As a variation on this recipe, make up a packet of mushroom soup to replace the water, and pour it over the mixture in the dish. This makes a delicious alternative.

Serves 4

RISSOLES

50 g (2 oz) breadcrumbs
1 egg, beaten
225 g (8 oz) minced beef
$^1/_4$ teaspoon salt
$^1/_4$ teaspoon mixed herbs
$^1/_4$ teaspoon lemon peel, grated
pepper
1 tablespoon vegetable oil

Mix the breadcrumbs, minced beef, herbs, lemon peel and seasoning and bind together with the beaten egg. Roll into rounds with lightly floured hands, and fry in the hot oil. Flatten with a fish slice into round flat rissole shapes. Cook slowly until brown on both sides.

Serves 3

Sausage and Courgette Provençale

50 g (2 oz) breadcrumbs
2 tablespoons water
225 g (8 oz) tomatoes, thinly sliced
2 or 3 courgettes, thinly sliced
1 medium onion, sliced into rings
450 g (1 lb) sausages
salt and pepper
1 teaspoon garlic paste

Layer the sliced vegetables in an ovenware dish, starting with a layer of tomatoes and flavouring each layer with a little salt and pepper mixed with the garlic paste. Pour over the water.

Prick the sausages with a fork and place on top of the vegetables in the dish. Sprinkle over the breadcrumbs. Cover with a lid and cook in a moderate oven (Gas Mark 4, 350°F, 180°C) for 1 hour. Remove the lid and continue cooking until the breadcrumbs are crisp and brown. Serve with boiled potatoes.

Serves 4

SAUSAGEMEAT: BEEF

225 g (8 oz) shoulder steak
50 g (2 oz) breadcrumbs
1 dessertspoon suet
1 teaspoon salt
pepper
pinch mixed spice
pinch oregano

Mince the beef and add to the breadcrumbs, suet, salt, pepper, oregano and a very little mixed spice. Mix well together, then pass once more through the mincing machine.

Use this delicious beef sausagemeat to fill pies or sausage rolls; cover with mashed or sliced potatoes and roast in the oven; form into rounds, dip in beaten egg, cover with breadcrumbs and fry to make beefburgers; make into meatballs and serve with tomato sauce on a bed of rice. It is also very tasty fried and eaten with hot toast as a breakfast dish.

Serves 4

SAUSAGEMEAT: MUTTON

450 g (1 lb) mutton (or stewing lamb)
100 g (4 oz) breadcrumbs
100 g (4 oz) suet
1 shallot, finely minced
1 teaspoon salt
pepper
nutmeg
2 eggs, beaten

Mince the mutton or lamb and mix with the breadcrumbs, suet, shallot, and season to taste. Pass the mixture through the mincing machine again. Blend in the well-beaten eggs.

See *Sausagemeat: Beef* for serving suggestions.

SAUSAGEMEAT: PORK

450 g (1 lb) fresh pork
100 g (4 oz) breadcrumbs
$^1/_2$ teaspoon dried sage
$^1/_2$ teaspoon dried onion
1 egg, beaten
salt and pepper

Mince the pork and add to the breadcrumbs, sage and onion, salt and pepper to taste. Mix in the beaten egg to form a stiff paste.

See *Sausagemeat: Beef* for serving suggestions.

Serves 4

Sausagemeat: Tomato

450 g (1 lb) minced beef
100 g (4 oz) breadcrumbs
1 tablespoon tomato purée
$1/2$ teaspoon salt
$1/4$ teaspoon pepper
1 teaspoon sugar
90 ml (3 fluid oz) boiling water

Place the breadcrumbs in a mixing bowl with the tomato purée and sugar. Pour on the boiling water, mix together and leave to go cold. Mix in the mincemeat and seasoning to form a stiff paste.

See *Sausagemeat: Beef* for serving suggestions.

Serves 4

Sausagemeat Trellis

50 g (2 oz) breadcrumbs
1 egg, beaten
225 g (8 oz) sausagemeat (see pages 140-143)
pinch dried onions
pinch sage
225 g (8 oz) puff pastry

Roll out the pastry and line a square tin or ovenware dish. Spread in the sausagemeat, sprinkle over a little dried onion and a pinch of sage. Pour over the breadcrumbs. Cut some strips of the remaining pastry to decorate the top in a trellis pattern. Brush the pastry with beaten egg to obtain a glaze finish. Cook for 30 minutes in a moderate oven (Gas Mark 4, 350°F, 180°C).

Serves 4

Sausages Oxford

225 g (8 oz) pork
225 g (8 oz) veal
100 g (4 oz) suet
100 g (4 oz) breadcrumbs
$^1/_2$ teaspoon sage
90 ml (3 fluid oz) water
salt and pepper
nutmeg

Mince together the pork and the veal. Mix with the suet, sage, salt and pepper to taste. Place the breadcrumbs in a basin and pour onto them the cold water. Mix well and leave to soak for about 10 minutes. Add the breadcrumb mixture to the other ingredients and mix well together.

See *Sausagemeat: Beef* for serving suggestions.

Serves 4

Savoury Ham Slice

450 g (1 lb) frying ham, cut thick
50 g (2 oz) breadcrumbs
1 tablespoon cooking oil
1 tablespoon brown sugar
1 small onion, finely chopped
$^1/_2$ teaspoon mustard powder
$^1/_2$ teaspoon paprika
90 ml (3 fluid oz) water

Cut the ham into slices, then lightly fry in oil on both sides. Remove from the pan and place in a shallow ovenware dish. Fry the chopped onion in the remaining hot fat for a few minutes. Add the mustard, sugar, paprika and water and bring to the boil. Pour over the ham. Sprinkle the breadcrumbs over the top and bake in a hot oven (Gas Mark 6, 400°F, 200°C) until golden brown.

Serves 3

SAVOURY MEAT BALLS

450 g (1 lb) minced beef
50 g (2 oz) breadcrumbs
1 egg, beaten
1 small onion, finely chopped
1 packet tomato soup, 1 cup size
knob of butter or margarine
270 ml (9 fluid oz) water
1 teaspoon salt
$^1/_4$ teaspoon pepper

Mix the minced beef with the breadcrumbs and bind with the beaten egg. With lightly floured hands, form the mixture into rounds. Fry the onion in the butter with the meat balls for a few minutes. Empty into the pan the packet of soup and the water. Place the lid firmly on the pan, and simmer for 30 minutes. Serve with rice.

Serves 4

SAVOURY PLATTER

50 g (2 oz) breadcrumbs
100 g (4 oz) grated cheese
1 tablespoon tomato purée
1 tablespoon water
knob butter or margarine
175 g (6 oz) unsweetened pastry

Roll out the pastry and use it to line a greased plate. Mix together the breadcrumbs and the cheese and sprinkle onto the pastry. Mix the purée with the water, pour over the breadcrumbs and top with pats of butter. Bake on the middle shelf of a hot oven (Gas Mark 6, 400°F, 200°C) until golden brown.

Serves 4

STEWED BEEF WITH MUSHROOMS

50 g (2 oz) breadcrumbs

450 g (1 lb) braising steak

6 fresh mushrooms, peeled and halved

1 tablespoon vegetable oil

600 ml (1 pint) water

salt and pepper

Heat the oil in a pan and brown the pieces of braising steak on both sides. Pour over the water, add the peeled and halved mushrooms and simmer gently for 1 hour. Add the breadcrumbs and season to taste. Continue cooking, stirring frequently, for a further 30 minutes until the meat is well cooked and tender. Serve on a hot dish with mushrooms around the edge.

Serves 4

TOMATOES WITH MINCED MEAT

50 g (2 oz) breadcrumbs
1 large onion, sliced into rings
1 x 400 g (14 oz) tin peeled tomatoes
225 g (8 oz) minced beef
1 tablespoon vegetable oil
300 ml ($\frac{1}{2}$ pint) water
$\frac{1}{2}$ teaspoon garlic paste
$\frac{1}{4}$ teaspoon oregano
salt and pepper

Heat the oil in a saucepan and fry the onion and the tomatoes. Add the minced beef and the water and bring to the boil. Turn the heat to very low and simmer for 30 minutes. Add the breadcrumbs and seasoning to taste and cook for a few more minutes to thicken. Pour onto a dish edged with mashed potatoes and serve hot.

Serves 2-4

SWEETS AND PUDDINGS

All good gifts around us
Are sent from heaven above;
Then thank the Lord,
O thank the Lord,
For all his love!

Matthias Claudius

ALMOND FLAN

50 g (2 oz) breadcrumbs
50 g (2 oz) ground almonds
2 dessertspoons raspberry jam
knob of butter
225 g (8 oz) shortcrust pastry
3 tablespoons icing sugar
2 drops almond essence

Grease and line an 8-inch sandwich tin with shortcrust pastry. Spread a layer of raspberry jam over the base. Mix half the ground almonds with the breadcrumbs and sprinkle onto the jam, levelling with a knife. Top with pats of butter. Cook on the middle shelf of a moderate oven (Gas Mark 4, 350°F, 180°C) for 30 minutes. Leave to go cold.

Mix together the remaining ground almonds with the icing sugar and drops of almond essence. Add a little water to make a spreading consistency. Pour over the top of the flan.

Serves 6-8

APPLE AND BLACKBERRY TART

50 g (2 oz) breadcrumbs
1 cooking apple, chopped
100 g (4 oz) blackberries
100 g (4 oz) sugar
knob of butter
175 g (6 oz) shortcrust pastry

Grease a 7-inch sandwich cake tin and line it with shortcrust pastry. Peel, core and chop the apples and place on the pastry base. Sprinkle on half the sugar, then the blackberries with the remaining sugar. Top with breadcrumbs and pats of butter. Bake for 40 minutes in a moderate oven, (Gas Mark 6, 400°F, 200°C) until golden.

Serves 4

APPLE BATTER

450 g (1 lb) cooking apples
100 g (4 oz) sugar
50 g (2 oz) breadcrumbs
100 g (4 oz) self raising flour
2 eggs, beaten
a pinch of powdered cloves (optional)

Peel and core the apples and place in a saucepan with just enough water to cover. Add the sugar and a pinch of powdered cloves. Cook for 10 minutes.

Butter liberally a pie dish. Sprinkle the sides and base with the breadcrumbs. Pour in the cooked apples. Beat well the eggs, and add to this the flour, beating to make a smooth batter. A little milk may be added if too dry. Pour over the apples, and cook in a hot oven (Gas Mark 6, 400°F, 200°C) for 30 minutes until crisp and golden.

Serves 4-5

APPLE CHARLOTTE

50 g (2 oz) breadcrumbs

450 g (1 lb) cooking apples, peeled and chopped

75 g (3 oz) sugar

juice and finely grated rind of ¹/₂ lemon

butter or margarine

Place the peeled, cored and chopped apples in an ovenware dish and sprinkle with sugar. Sprinkle the lemon rind on top, then add the strained juice. Spread the breadcrumbs over the top and add a few pats of butter. Cook in a moderate oven (Gas Mark 4, 350°F, 180°C) for 30 minutes. Serve with custard or with cream.

Serves 4

APPLE DUMPLINGS

100 g (4 oz) suet pastry
2 cooking apples, peeled and cored
50 g (2 oz) breadcrumbs
1 tablespoon brown sugar
2 cloves
butter or margarine

Roll out the suet pastry and cut into saucer-sized rounds. Put a clove in each apple, add a pat of butter, then fill to the top with the mixed breadcrumbs and sugar.

Place an apple on each pastry round, wet the edges of the pastry and gather up to enclose the apples. Place the apple dumplings on a greased baking tray with the best side up. Brush the pastry with milk, sprinkle with sugar and bake in a hot oven (Gas Mark 5, 375°F, 190°C) for 25 minutes for a very satisfying pudding.

Serves 2

APPLE FLAN

50 g (2 oz) breadcrumbs
100 g (4 oz) sugar
2 apples
2 tablespoons water
$\frac{1}{2}$ teaspoon cinnamon
2 tablespoons raspberry jam
225 g (8 oz) shortcrust pastry

Line a flan dish with shortcrust pastry, spread some raspberry jam onto the base, and sprinkle in the breadcrumbs. Peel and core the apples, cut into thin slices and decorate the top with these. Put the sugar and cinnamon into a basin, add the water and mix together. Spoon the damp sugar on top of the apples. Bake for 1 hour in a moderate oven (Gas Mark 4, 350°F, 180°C) or until the sugar has turned to syrup.

Serves 4-6

APPLE PIE

50 g (2 oz) breadcrumbs
75 g (3 oz) brown sugar
450 g (1 lb) cooking apples, peeled, cored and sliced
1 lemon
175 g (6 oz) shortcrust pastry
1 teaspoon castor sugar

Place a layer of sliced apples in a pie dish and sprinkle with a little grated lemon rind and some of the sugar and breadcrumbs. Continue to layer the ingredients until the dish is filled, ending with a layer of apples. Pour over the strained juice of the lemon and a very little water to moisten. Roll out the pastry thinly and cover, brushing with a little milk and sprinkling with a teaspoon of sugar. Bake in a moderate oven (Gas Mark 3, 325°F, 170°C) for 1 hour.

Serves 4

APPLE PUDDING

50 g (2 oz) breadcrumbs

225 g (8 oz) cooking apples, peeled, cored
and sliced

100 g (4 oz) self raising flour

175 g (6 oz) sugar

100 g (4 oz) soft margarine

1 egg and milk to make 150 ml (5 fluid oz)

1 level teaspoon baking powder

$^1/_2$ teaspoon salt

a pinch of powdered cloves (optional)

Cream together the margarine and half of the sugar in a mixing bowl and then add the flour, salt and baking powder. Pour in the beaten egg and milk and stir well together. Finally, mix in the breadcrumbs.

Mix the remaining sugar with the powdered cloves and the sliced apples and place in a large basin. Cover with the breadcrumb mixture, and tie greaseproof paper over the top. Place in a large pan with boiling water reaching half-way up the basin. Simmer gently for $1^1/_2$ hours. Delicious with hot custard.

Serves 6

APRICOT CREAM

1 x 400 g (14 oz) tin apricots
50 g (2 oz) breadcrumbs
2 eggs plus two extra yolks
420 ml (14 fluid oz) milk
50 g (2 oz) sugar
3 drops vanilla essence
1 small carton fresh whipping cream

Strain the apricots and bring the juice to the boil in a saucepan. Turn off the heat, stir in the breadcrumbs, and pour into an 8-inch ovenware dish. Cover with the apricots.

Whisk well together the eggs, the extra yolks, vanilla essence and sugar. Boil the milk and pour into the egg mixture. Beat well together then pour slowly over the apricots in the dish. Place the dish in a tray of hot water and cook in a moderate oven (Gas Mark 4, 350°F, 180°C) for about 45 minutes, until set. Remove from the oven and put a plate on top to prevent a hard skin forming. Leave in the refrigerator to go very cold.

Whip the fresh cream until stiff and spread over the top before serving. For a special occasion, pipe on the cream and decorate with flaked almonds.

Serves 7

Apricot Flan

1 x 400 g (14 oz) tin apricot halves

2 dessertspoons sugar

1 dessertspoon cornflour

50 g (2 oz) breadcrumbs

175 g (6 oz) shortcrust pastry

Put the cornflour into a basin with just enough water to flake it. Strain the apricot halves. Measure the juice and make up to 8 fluid oz with water. Pour into a saucepan, and add 1 dessertspoon of sugar. Boil, and pour the cornflour over it, stirring until it thickens. Remove from the heat then stir in the breadcrumbs. Beat well together and leave to go cool. Line an 8-inch sandwich cake tin with shortcrust pastry and spread in the mixture, decorating the top with the halved apricots. Sprinkle over the second dessertspoon of sugar. Bake for 45 minutes at Gas Mark 6, 400°F, 200°C.

Serves 4-6

APRICOT MERINGUE

100 g (4 oz) sugar
25 g (1 oz) breadcrumbs
50 g (2 oz) self raising flour
2 eggs, separated
1 x 400 g (14 oz) tin apricot halves
225 g (8 oz) shortcrust pastry
2 tablespoons castor sugar

Line a deep sandwich cake tin with shortcrust pastry. Drain the apricots. Process half the fruit and half the sugar in a blender or liquidizer and pour the resulting purée into the pastry case. Beat together the breadcrumbs, flour, the remaining sugar and the yolks of the eggs. Pour over the fruit purée. Whip the egg whites to a stiff consistency with the castor sugar and spoon onto the mixture. Decorate the top with the remaining apricots and cook in a medium hot oven (Gas Mark 5, 375°F, 190°C) for about 40 minutes or until the meringue has turned golden.

Serves 6

Autumn Pudding

50 g (2 oz) breadcrumbs

1 cooking apple, peeled, cored and finely chopped

2 eggs, beaten

200 ml (¹/₃ pint) milk

1 tablespoon demerara sugar

6 slices bread and butter

Chop a good, sharp cooking apple and mix with the sugar. Remove the crusts from some slices of buttered bread and sandwich together with a filling of apples and sugar. Cut into squares and place in a greased ovenware dish.

Beat the eggs and add the milk so that the two are combined together before pouring the liquid over the squares of bread. Leave for a few minutes for the liquid to soak into the bread. Cover with the breadcrumbs and bake in a low oven (Gas Mark 2, 300°F, 150°C) for 30 minutes.

Serves 3

BLACKBERRY AND APPLE CRUMBLE

1 large cooking apple, peeled, cored and chopped
225 g (8 oz) blackberries
2 tablespoons water
100 g (4 oz) sugar
100 g (4 oz) breadcrumbs
butter or margarine

Place in an ovenware dish the blackberries and apples mixed with the sugar. Sprinkle on a little water. Cover with breadcrumbs and top with pats of butter or margarine. Cook in a moderate oven (Gas Mark 4, 350°F, 180°C) for 30 minutes.

Serves 4

BLACKBERRY JELLY AND APPLE TART

50 g (2 oz) breadcrumbs
2 cooking apples, peeled, cored and grated
50 g (2 oz) sugar
2 tablespoons blackberry jelly
butter or margarine
225 g (8 oz) shortcrust pastry

Grease a sandwich cake tin and line it with shortcrust pastry. Spread the base with blackberry jelly. Grate the apples and spread onto the jelly. Sprinkle with the sugar, then the breadcrumbs, and top with pats of butter. Bake for 40 minutes in a moderate oven (Gas Mark 4, 350°F, 180°C).

Serves 4

BLACKBERRY PIE

50 g (2 oz) breadcrumbs
450 g (1 lb) blackberries
100 g (4 oz) sugar
100 g (4 oz) shortcrust pastry

Grease well a pie dish and sprinkle in the breadcrumbs, then the blackberries and finally the sugar. Cover the pie with shortcrust pastry, brushed with a little milk to glaze. Bake for 30 minutes in a moderate oven (Gas Mark 4, 350°F, 180°C).

Serves 4-6

BLACKCURRANT CRUMBLE

100 g (4 oz) breadcrumbs

350 g (12 oz) blackcurrants, fresh or frozen

175 g (6 oz) sugar

90 ml (3 fluid oz) water

butter or margarine

Place in an ovenware dish the blackcurrants, sugar and water. Sprinkle the breadcrumbs on top and cover with pats of butter. Bake in a moderate oven (Gas Mark 4, 350°F, 180°C) for 30 minutes. Serve with custard.

Serves 4

BLACKCURRANT MOULD

50 g (2 oz) breadcrumbs
1 small tin blackcurrants
100 g (4 oz) sugar
1 tablespoon boiling water
1 tablespoon powdered gelatine

Drain the blackcurrants, reserving the juice, and place in a liquidizer. Dissolve the gelatine in a tablespoon of hot water and make up to 6 fluid oz with the reserved juice. Pour into the liquidizer and add the sugar and breadcrumbs. Process until smooth, then pour into a basin or mould to set.

Blackcurrant mould is excellent served with whipped cream.

Serves 3

BRANDY PUDDING

100 g (4 oz) breadcrumbs
1 dessertspoon sunflower oil
25 g (1 oz) butter
50 g (2 oz) sugar
2 tablespoons brandy
2 eggs, beaten
200 ml (¹/₃ pint) hot milk
nutmeg
salt

Place the breadcrumbs, butter and oil in a bowl and pour over the boiled milk. Mix well and leave to go cold. Add the beaten eggs, sugar, salt and a grating of nutmeg. Finally mix in the brandy. Pour into a well-greased 6¹/₂-inch soufflé dish and bake in a moderate to low oven (Gas Mark 3, 325°F, 170°C) for 30 minutes.

Serves 4

BREAD AND JAM PUDDING

100 g (4 oz) breadcrumbs
2 dessertspoons jam
2 eggs, beaten
200 ml (¹/₃ pint) milk
1 dessertspoon sugar

Place half the jam in a buttered pudding basin and cover with half the breadcrumbs. Spoon in the remaining jam and cover with the rest of the breadcrumbs. Break the eggs into a basin, add the milk and sugar and beat well together. Pour over the bread and jam in the basin and leave to soak in. Cover with buttered paper, tie down with string and steam for 45 minutes.

This pudding is excellent served with hot custard or with ice cream.

Serves 3

CABINET PUDDING

100 g (4 oz) breadcrumbs
360 ml (12 fluid oz) milk
2 eggs, beaten
1 tablespoon sugar
salt
cinnamon
14 seedless raisins
butter

Beat the eggs and the milk together and pour over the crumbs in a mixing bowl. Add the sugar, a pinch of salt and a pinch of cinnamon. Leave a little while to soak.

Spread a basin thickly with butter and press the seedless raisins into the base and sides. Pour in the crumb mixture, cover with buttered paper and steam gently for 1 hour for a really tasty pudding.

Serves 4

CARAMEL APPLE PUDDING

2 medium cooking apples, peeled, cored and chopped
50 g (2 oz) breadcrumbs
100 g (4 oz) sugar
50 g (2 oz) raisins
1 tablespoon dark brown sugar
butter
350 g (12 oz) shortcrust pastry

Generously grease a large pudding basin and coat with butter and brown sugar. Roll out the pastry thinly and line the basin with it. Fill with layers of apples, breadcrumbs and raisins and a sprinkling of sugar. Add a little water to moisten. Cut out a ring of pastry for a lid, wet the edges and seal neatly. Bake in a moderate oven (Gas Mark 4, 350°F, 180°C) for 1 hour or until golden. Turn out and serve with hot custard.

Serves 4-6

CHOCOLATE PUDDING

225 g (8 oz) breadcrumbs
450 ml (³/₄ pint) hot milk
100 g (4 oz) sugar
1 tablespoon cocoa
1 tablespoon cooking oil
2 eggs, separated

Place the breadcrumbs in a mixing bowl and pour over the hot milk. Leave to go cold. Pour into a blender and add the cocoa, sugar, oil and the yolks of the eggs. Mix well together.

Beat the egg whites until frothy. Pour the crumb mixture into a greased ovenware dish and fold in the egg whites. Bake in a moderate oven (Gas Mark 4, 350°F, 180°C) for 35 minutes. Serve sprinkled with castor sugar.

Serves 4

Chocolate Trifle

For the chocolate sponge

50 g (2 oz) breadcrumbs

175 g (6 oz) soft margarine

175 g (6 oz) sugar

100 g (4 oz) self raising flour

1 egg

3 tablespoons milk

1 tablespoon cocoa

1 teaspoon baking powder

salt

bicarbonate of soda

black cherry jam

1 wineglassful brandy

For the chocolate sauce

2 tablespoons cornflour

600 ml (1 pint) milk

1 tablespoon cocoa

25 g (1 oz) butter

50 g (2 oz) sugar

3 drops vanilla essence

To decorate

1 small carton whipping cream

2 tablespoons walnuts, chopped

6 glucé cherries, halved

Process all the sponge ingredients in a mixer until smooth. Add a little extra milk if necessary. Bake in an 8-inch cake tin lined with buttered paper for 30 minutes at Gas Mark 4, 350°F, 180°C. Allow to cool.

Spread in the base of a trifle dish a generous layer of black cherry jam. Place on top of this the sliced chocolate cake and pour over the brandy. Allow to soak in.

To make the chocolate sauce, mix the cornflour, cocoa and sugar with a very little of the milk. Pour the remainder into a saucepan and bring to the boil. Remove from the heat and stir in the cornflour mixture. Add the butter and a few drops of vanilla essence and return to the heat for a few minutes, stirring constantly until thick and creamy. Remove from the heat and allow to cool a little Spoon the chocolate sauce over the cake in the trifle dish. Cover with a clean damp cloth to prevent a skin forming and leave in a cool place to set.

Cover the top with fresh whipped cream and decorate with chopped walnuts and glacé cherries.

Serves 8

CHRISTMAS PUDDING

100 g (4 oz) breadcrumbs
225 g (8 oz) self raising flour
50 g (2 oz) suet
175 g (6 oz) sugar
1 carrot, grated
100 g (4 oz) currants
100 g (4 oz) sultanas
100 g (4 oz) raisins
50 g (2 oz) chopped peel
50 g (2 oz) chopped almonds
1 tablespoon treacle
3 tablespoons hot milk
juice and finely grated rind of 1 lemon
1 tablespoon rum
3 eggs, beaten
$\frac{1}{4}$ teaspoon salt
$\frac{1}{4}$ teaspoon nutmeg
$\frac{1}{4}$ teaspoon mixed spice
$\frac{1}{4}$ teaspoon ground ginger

Mix together the dry ingredients, the grated carrot and the lemon juice and rind. Add the mixed milk and treacle, then the rum and the well-beaten eggs. Mix well before adding the fruit and nuts. Stir well in, adding a small amount of water if a little dry. Pour into a buttered pudding basin, cover with buttered paper and tie down. Steam for 2½ hours in a saucepan of water, or steam for 20 minutes then pressure-cook for 1 hour. This recipe makes a delicious moist and fruity pudding.

Coconut Pudding

100 g (4 oz) breadcrumbs
50 g (2 oz) desiccated coconut
175 g (6 oz) sugar
50 g (2 oz) butter, melted
1 large egg, beaten
200 ml ($^1/_3$ pint) milk
1 teaspoon lemon rind, grated
100 g (4 oz) self raising flour

Beat well together the egg and milk, and add the sugar and melted butter. Stir in the coconut, breadcrumbs and grated lemon peel. Add a little more milk if the mixture feels too dry. Steam for 2 hours in a greased pudding basin covered with greaseproof paper and then tied down with string.

Serves 4-6

COLLEGE PUDDING

50 g (2 oz) breadcrumbs
100 g (4 oz) self raising flour
100 g (4 oz) suet
100 g (4 oz) currants
100 g (4 oz) mixed dried fruit
75 g (3 oz) brown sugar
2 eggs, beaten
2 tablespoons milk
$^{1}/_{2}$ teaspoon salt
$^{1}/_{2}$ teaspoon bicarbonate of soda
$^{1}/_{2}$ teaspoon mixed spice

Mix together all the dry ingredients in a bowl. Beat the eggs and mix into the bowl, adding the milk to obtain a soft dropping consistency.

Steam for 2 hours in a well-greased pudding basin and serve with hot custard.

Serves 4-6

Fig Pudding

50 g (2 oz) breadcrumbs
100 g (4 oz) self raising flour
100 g (4 oz) butter or soft margarine
100 g (4 oz) brown sugar
100 g (4 oz) figs, chopped
1 egg, beaten
150 ml ($^1/_4$ pint) milk
1 tablespoon lemon juice

Cream together the sugar and butter and mix in the flour and breadcrumbs. Add the egg and milk and beat well together. Lastly, stir in the figs and lemon juice. Pour into a well-greased basin, cover with buttered paper and tie down with string. Steam for at least 1 hour and serve with hot custard.

Serves 4

FRUIT PLATE TART

50 g (2 oz) breadcrumbs

1 large cooking apple, peeled, cored and sliced

juice and finely grated rind of 1 lemon

1 tablespoon water

50 g (2 oz) raisins

50 g (2 oz) sultanas

100 g (4 oz) sugar

175 g (6 oz) shortcrust pastry

Cook the sliced apple in a covered saucepan with the sugar, lemon juice and rind, and a tablespoon of water. When tender, allow to cool.

Butter an ovenproof dinner plate and cover with shortcrust pastry. Spread over the apple slices, sprinkle on the sultanas and raisins and top with breadcrumbs. Bake in a hot oven (Gas Mark 6, 400°F, 200°C) for 20 minutes.

Serves 4-6

GOOSEBERRY AND RICE PUDDING

50 g (2 oz) white rice

600 ml (1 pint) water plus 2 tablespoons

350 g (12 oz) green gooseberries

100 g (4 oz) sugar

$^1/_2$ teaspoon lemon rind, grated

knob butter

salt

Wash the rice and place in a pan with a pint of water and a pinch of salt. Simmer gently for 20 minutes until just cooked. Strain away the water then place half the rice in a buttered pie dish. Add half the gooseberries and sprinkle with the sugar mixed with the grated lemon rind. Add a second layer of boiled rice, gooseberries and sugar and finish with a layer of rice. Pour over 2 tablespoons water, cover with breadcrumbs and a few pats of butter. Bake for 45 minutes in a moderate oven (Gas Mark 4, 350°F, 180°C). Gooseberry and rice pudding is excellent served with a hot egg custard.

Serves 6

GOOSEBERRY CRUNCH

225 g (8 oz) gooseberries

50 g (2 oz) breadcrumbs

100 g (4 oz) sugar

150 ml (1/4 pint) water

butter or margarine

Place the gooseberries in an ovenware dish and pour over the sugar and water. Add the breadcrumbs, and top with pats of butter or margarine. Cook in a medium hot oven (Gas Mark 4, 350°F, 180°C) for 15 minutes until golden brown. Delicious served hot or cold with evaporated milk or ice cream.

Serves 2-4

GOOSEBERRY MERINGUE

175 g (6 oz) gooseberries
200 ml (¹/₃ pint) water
50 g (2 oz) breadcrumbs
100 g (4 oz) sugar
2 egg whites
100 g (4 oz) castor sugar
1 small carton whipping cream

Cook the gooseberries, sugar and water in a saucepan until tender. Stir in the breadcrumbs and pour the mixture into a pie dish.

Whisk the egg whites with the castor sugar until they stand up in peaks. Spoon onto the top of the gooseberry mixture. Cook in a warm oven (Gas Mark 3, 325°F, 170°C) for 40 minutes, until the meringue is cooked. Allow to go cold before spreading some stiffly whipped cream over the top.

Serves 4-5

GOOSEBERRY SURPRISE

50 g (2 oz) breadcrumbs
225 g (8 oz) gooseberries
100 g (4 oz) sugar
2 tablespoons water

Cook together the gooseberries, water and sugar until tender. Layer the gooseberries and breadcrumbs in a mould until all are used up, ending with a layer of breadcrumbs. Leave overnight in the refrigerator. Serve with fresh cream.

Serves 4

GOOSEBERRY TART

50 g (2 oz) breadcrumbs

100 g (4 oz) sugar

350 g (12 oz) gooseberries

175 g (6 oz) shortcrust pastry

Grease a sandwich cake tin and line it with shortcrust pastry. Fill with the gooseberries. If fresh gooseberries are used, moisten the sugar with 2 tablespoons of water and sprinkle onto the gooseberries. If using frozen gooseberries, there is no need to defrost before sprinkling with the dry sugar. Cover with the bread-crumbs. Place in a hot oven (Gas Mark 6, 400°F, 200°C) and cook for 30 minutes.

At the end of the cooking time, press with a fork to level the top and to test the gooseberries. Place back in the oven for a further 15 minutes until the breadcrumbs and pastry turn golden.

This gooseberry tart is very good with evaporated milk.

Serves 4

Lemon Plate Tart

2 oz breadcrumbs

juice and finely grated rind of 1 large lemon

50 g (2 oz) sugar

210 ml (7 fluid oz) boiling water

25 g (1 oz) butter

1 tablespoon cornflour

1 egg, beaten

250 ml (10 oz) shortcrust pastry

Line an ovenproof dinner plate with shortcrust pastry. Moisten the cornflour with a very little water, then pour onto it the boiling water. Stir well and add the lemon rind and the strained lemon juice, the butter, sugar and lastly the well-beaten egg. Pour onto the pastry and sprinkle the top with breadcrumbs. Bake in a moderate oven (Gas Mark 4, 350°F, 180°C) for 1 hour.

MAID OF HONOUR

400 ml (²/₃ pint) milk
75 g (3 oz) breadcrumbs
75 g (3 oz) butter
75 g (3 oz) sugar
3 eggs, beaten
grated rind of ¹/₂ lemon
175 g (6 oz) shortcrust pastry
4 tablespoons lemon curd

Bring to the boil the milk mixed with the breadcrumbs, butter, sugar and the lemon rind. Turn the heat down and continue cooking for 5 minutes. Add the beaten eggs to the mixture in the pan and turn off the heat. Stir until it thickens. Line a sandwich cake tin with the pastry and pour in the mixture. Bake in a hot oven (Gas Mark 6, 400°F, 200°C) for 50 minutes. Allow to cool and spread the top with lemon curd before serving.

Serves 4

MARMALADE DELIGHT

50 g (2 oz) breadcrumbs

2 eggs, beaten

300 ml (¹/₂ pint) milk

grated rind of ¹/₂ lemon

2-4 tablespoons marmalade

1 dessertspoon sugar

175 g (6 oz) sweet shortcrust pastry

Line a buttered pie dish with sweet shortcrust pastry and spread marmalade to taste over the base. Beat the eggs well with half a pint of fresh milk, and add to this the breadcrumbs and a little grated lemon rind. Pour this into the pastry case and sprinkle the top with sugar. Bake for 45 minutes in a moderate oven (Gas Mark 4, 350°F, 180°C). Serve hot with cream.

Serves 4

MARMALADE PUDDING

50 g (2 oz) breadcrumbs
200 ml (¹/₃ pint) hot milk
1 tablespoon sugar
1 tablespoon butter
2 eggs, separated
2-4 tablespoons marmalade
3 drops vanilla essence
1 tablespoon castor sugar

Put into a bowl the breadcrumbs, sugar, butter and a few drops of vanilla essence. Pour over the hot milk, add the beaten egg yolks and stir well into the mixture. Pour into a buttered ovenware dish and bake for 30 minutes in a moderate oven (Gas Mark 4, 350°F, 180°C).

When cool, cover with marmalade. Beat the egg whites with the castor sugar until stiff and spread the meringue over the marmalade. Return the marmalade pudding to a cool oven (Gas Mark 1, 275°F, 140°C) for 30-40 minutes, to crisp.

Serves 4

Marmalade Trellis Square

25 g (1 oz) breadcrumbs
175 g (6 oz) puff pastry
2 tablespoons marmalade
1 egg, beaten

Roll out enough puff pastry to cover a square or oblong baking tin, leaving some over to form a trellis to decorate the top. Spread the base with the marmalade and cover with the breadcrumbs and then the strips of pastry. Brush the pastry generously with the beaten egg and cook in a hot oven (Gas Mark 6, 400°F, 200°C) until golden. Serve hot with a little whipped cream.

Serves 6

ORANGE SNOW PUDDING

100 g (4 oz) breadcrumbs
400 ml (^{2}/$_3$ pint) hot milk
225 g (8 oz) castor sugar
4 eggs, separated
juice and finely grated rind of 2 oranges
knob of butter or margarine

Mix together the breadcrumbs, butter, orange rind and half of the sugar. Pour over these the hot milk and stir until well blended. Add the strained orange juice and stir in the beaten egg yolks. Pour the mixture into a buttered ovenware dish and bake for 30 minutes in a moderate oven (Gas Mark 4, 350°F, 180°C).

Whisk the egg whites with the remaining sugar until stiff. Pile onto the top of the pudding and continue cooking until set at Gas Mark 2, 200°F, 150°C.

Serves 4

PEACH FLAN

100 g (4 oz) castor sugar
1 medium tin sliced peaches
25 g (1 oz) breadcrumbs
1 tablespoon cornflour
2 eggs, separated
300 ml (10 fluid oz) fruit juice and water
1 dessertspoon granulated sugar
3 drops vanilla essence

Drain the juice from the peaches and reserve. Lay the peach slices on the bottom of an oven-ware dish, keeping a few for decoration. Mix the cornflour with a little of the peach juice. Pour the remainder into a saucepan and bring to the boil before adding the moistened cornflour. Mix well, then add the breadcrumbs, granulated sugar and the vanilla essence, and the yolks from the eggs, one at a time. Beat well together and pour this mixture over the fruit in the dish.

Whisk the egg whites with the castor sugar until the meringue stands in peaks. Spoon onto the top of the mixture, adding a few peach slices for decoration. Cook in a moderate oven (Gas Mark 4, 350°F, 180°C) for 40 minutes, until set.

Serves 6

Plum Charlotte

100 g (4 oz) breadcrumbs
450 g (1 lb) Victoria plums
100 g (4 oz) demerara sugar
200 ml (¹/₃ pint) water

Line a buttered ovenware dish with half the breadcrumbs. Place the plums in a pan with the water and sugar, and cook very gently, keeping the fruit whole. Lay the plums in the dish, and pour over the juice. Cover the top with the remainder of the breadcrumbs. Bake for 20 minutes in a hot oven (Gas Mark 6, 400°F, 200°C). Serve cold with fresh cream.

Serves 4

PLUM PUDDING, RICH

225 g (8 oz) breadcrumbs
175 g (6 oz) sugar
100 g (4 oz) self raising flour
50 g (2 oz) sultanas
50 g (2 oz) raisins
50 g (2 oz) currants
50 g (2 oz) mixed peel
50 g (2 oz) cherries
50 g (2 oz) suet
50 g (2 oz) almonds, chopped
2 large eggs
1 tablespoon milk
$\frac{1}{2}$ teaspoon mixed spice
$\frac{1}{2}$ teaspoon baking powder
$\frac{1}{2}$ teaspoon salt

Mix together all the dry ingredients. Beat together the eggs with the milk and stir in until well blended. Add a little extra milk if the mixture seems too dry. Pour into a buttered pudding basin, cover with buttered paper and tie down with string. Steam for $2\frac{1}{2}$ hours. Serve with hot custard.

Serves 8

PRUNE CRUNCH

450 g (1 lb) prunes
juice and finely grated rind of $\frac{1}{2}$ lemon
50 g (2 oz) breadcrumbs
50 g (2 oz) sugar
1 dessertspoon cornflour
1 tablespoon water
600 ml (1 pint) strained tea

Wash the prunes and place in a large basin. Pour over the strained tea and allow to cool. Cover with a plate and leave overnight to soak.

Fill a saucepan with the soaked prunes and the liquid, add the sugar, then the lemon juice and rind. Bring to the boil then simmer gently for 30 minutes.

Flake the cornflour with a tablespoon of water and mix well. Stir into the prunes, turn off the heat and stir until the mixture thickens. Pour into an ovenware dish, sprinkle with breadcrumbs and brown for 10 minutes in a hot oven (Gas Mark 6, 400°F, 200°C) or crisp under a hot grill. Serve with hot custard.

Serves 4

QUICKLY SWEET

50 g (2 oz) breadcrumbs

225 g (8 oz) raspberry or strawberry jam

300 ml (¹/₂ pint) custard

Butter an ovenware dish and spread the base with a thick layer of jam. Sprinkle on top the breadcrumbs, level them with a spoon and cover with the ready-made custard. Cook for 20 minutes in a cool oven (Gas Mark 2, 300°F, 150°C). This makes a very simple and quick sweet course that young and old alike enjoy. It's also a good way to use up left-over custard.

Serves 4

RASPBERRY DELIGHT

50 g (2 oz) breadcrumbs
225 g (8 oz) fresh raspberries
175 g (6 oz) sugar

Layer in a basin the raspberries, sugar, and breadcrumbs until all the ingredients are used, ending with a layer of breadcrumbs. Place on top of the basin a plate or saucer, adding a heavy weight to press all together. Leave overnight in the refrigerator. Turn out and serve with fresh cream.

Serves 4

RASPBERRY MERINGUE

50 g (2 oz) breadcrumbs
2 eggs, separated
2 tablespoons raspberry jam
100 g (4 oz) castor sugar
1 tablespoon milk
2 drops almond essence
butter or margarine

Butter a 6-inch soufflé dish and spread the base with raspberry jam. Beat together the egg yolks, milk and almond essence and mix in the breadcrumbs. Spread the mixture over the jam.

Whisk the egg whites, add half the sugar and whisk again. Add the remaining sugar and whisk until the mixture stands up in peaks. Spoon on top of the mixture in the soufflé dish and bake for 40 minutes at Gas Mark 2, 300°F, 150°C.

Raspberry meringue can be eaten hot, or is delicious cold served with cream.

Serves 4

RHUBARB AND LEMON CRUMBLE

---

100 g (4 oz) breadcrumbs

---

450 g (1 lb) rhubarb, cut into 1-inch pieces

---

175 g (6 oz) brown sugar

---

150 ml ($^1/_4$ pint) water

---

juice and finely grated rind of $^1/_2$ lemon

Pour the water into a saucepan and bring to the boil. Add the lemon juice and rind, the rhubarb and the sugar. Simmer together for a few minutes, so that the rhubarb remains whole. Pour into a buttered ovenware dish and cover the top with breadcrumbs. Bake for 15 minutes in a hot oven (Gas Mark 6, 400°F, 200°C) until golden. Serve with hot custard.

Serves 4-6

RHUBARB AND STRAWBERRY MOULD

50 g (2 oz) breadcrumbs

175 g (6 oz) rhubarb, cut into 1-inch pieces

175 g (6 oz) sugar

200 ml (⅓ pint) water

1 tablet strawberry jelly

1 small tin evaporated milk

Place the chopped rhubarb in a saucepan with the sugar and water. Cook for a few minutes until the rhubarb becomes tender. Stir in the breadcrumbs, turn off the heat, and mix well together. Remove from the heat and add the jelly, stirring until completely dissolved. Pour in the evaporated milk, mix well, then pour into a jelly mould to set.

Serves 4-6

SHERRY PUDDING

175 g (6 oz) breadcrumbs
175 g (6 oz) castor sugar
100 g (4 oz) sultanas
200 ml (1/3 pint) milk
1 tablespoon candied peel
50 g (1 oz) granulated sugar
1 teaspoon water
grated rind of 1/2 lemon
2 egg yolks
1 tablespoon sherry

Mix together the breadcrumbs, sugar, sultanas, candied peel and lemon rind. Pour 1 oz of granulated sugar into a saucepan with a teaspoon of water. Place on a low heat and stir constantly until it becomes dark in colour and caramelized. Pour in the milk and bring to the boil until the sugar dissolves in it.

When cold, blend in the egg yolks and a tablespoon of sherry. Mix with the dry ingredients and pour into a well-buttered pudding basin. Steam for 1 hour.

Serves 6

STEAMED LEMON PUDDING

100 g (4 oz) breadcrumbs
100 g (4 oz) self raising flour
100 g (4 oz) margarine
175 g (6 oz) sugar
juice and finely grated rind of 1 lemon
2 eggs, beaten

Cream the sugar and margarine and gradually mix in the breadcrumbs, flour, lemon juice and rind. Stir in the beaten eggs and mix well. Pour into a buttered pudding basin, cover with buttered paper and tie down with string. Steam for $1^{1}/_{2}$ hours. Serve with hot custard or lemon sauce.

Serves 4

STEWED APPLE PUDDING

450 g (1 lb) cooking apples, peeled, cored and chopped
50 g (2 oz) breadcrumbs
100 g (4 oz) sugar
600 ml (1 pint) milk
2 eggs, separated
25 g (1 oz) butter
½ teaspoon vanilla essence

Cook the chopped apples with half the sugar and just enough water to cover until tender. Pour into a buttered pie dish.

Melt the butter in a saucepan, add the breadcrumbs, then gradually stir in the milk. Simmer together for 2 minutes. Pour the mixture into a bowl and add to this the remaining sugar and the vanilla essence. Allow to cool a little before beating in the egg yolks one at a time to thicken.

Whisk the egg whites to a stiff froth then fold into the crumb mixture. Pour over the stewed apples in the pie dish and bake for 45 minutes in a moderate oven (Gas Mark 4, 350°F, 180°C) until risen.

Serves 4

Syrup Pudding

50 g (2 oz) breadcrumbs
100 g (4 oz) self raising flour
175 g (6 oz) butter or margarine
75 g (3 oz) sugar
1 egg
2 tablespoons milk
1 teaspoon ground ginger
3 tablespoons golden syrup

Cream the butter and sugar, stir in the flour then the breadcrumbs and ginger. Beat together the egg and milk and stir into the mixture. Warm a tablespoon in boiling water then measure the syrup into a greased pudding basin. Pour the crumb mixture on top of the syrup. Cover with buttered paper, tie down with string and steam for 1 hour. This syrup pudding is delicious served with hot custard.

Serves 4

TREACLE TART

50 g (2 oz) breadcrumbs
3 tablespoons golden syrup
knob of butter
175 g (6 oz) shortcrust pastry

Grease a 7-inch sandwich tin and line it with shortcrust pastry. Pour into this the syrup, cover with breadcrumbs and top with pats of butter. Cook for 30 minutes in a moderate oven (Gas Mark 4, 350°F, 180°C) until golden brown. Serve warm with fresh unsweetened cream.

Serves 4

CAKES AND COOKIES

Our Father, for our daily bread
Accept our praise and hear our prayer
By thee all living souls are fed
Thy bounty and thy loving care
With all thy children let us share.

G.W. Briggs

APPLE AND GINGER CAKE

225 g (8 oz) self raising flour

50 g (2 oz) breadcrumbs

175 g (6 oz) sugar

175 g (6 oz) butter or margarine

1 cooking apple, peeled, cored and finely chopped

50 g (2 oz) preserved ginger, finely cut

2 teaspoons ground ginger

1 teaspoon baking powder

200 ml (1/3 pint) milk

2 eggs, beaten

Cream together the butter and sugar and add the beaten eggs and the milk. Beat well together, adding a little flour to prevent curdling. Add the breadcrumbs, flour and baking powder and mix well before adding the ginger and the finely chopped apple. Pour into a cake tin lined with buttered paper. Bake in a moderate oven (Gas Mark 4, 350°F, 180°C) for 1 hour, or until it will not leave an indent when pressed with a finger.

Serves 6-8

APPLE CAKE

3 dessert apples, peeled, cored and chopped

225 g (8 oz) self raising flour

50 g (2 oz) breadcrumbs

175 g (6 oz) granulated sugar

175 g (6 oz) soft margarine

1 teaspoon baking powder

1 egg

200 ml (1/3 pint) milk

1 teaspoon vanilla essence

1 teaspoon brown sugar

salt

Stir together the flour, breadcrumbs, sugar, baking powder and salt, then add the margarine and mix well in. Put the egg, milk and vanilla essence into a blender and process before adding to the ingredients in the bowl. Cut the apples into big chunks and add to the mixture. Pour into a cake tin lined with buttered paper and sprinkle a teaspoon of brown sugar on the top. Bake for 1½ hours in a moderate oven (Gas Mark 4, 350°F, 180°C).

Serves 6

APRICOT AND VANILLA CAKE

50 g (2 oz) breadcrumbs

175 g (6 oz) soft margarine

175 g (6 oz) sugar

100 g (4 oz) self raising flour

2 eggs, beaten

1 tablespoon milk

3 drops vanilla essence

For the topping and filling

75 g (3 oz) soft margarine

75 g (3 oz) icing sugar

$^1/_2$ teaspoon vanilla essence

1 dessertspoon milk

4 tablespoons apricot jam

100 g (4 oz) chopped nuts

To make the cake, cream together the margarine and the sugar, add a little flour, then beat in the eggs, vanilla essence and the milk. Add the remaining flour and the breadcrumbs. If the mixture is too moist, add an extra spoonful of flour to form a dropping consistency. Line a 6-inch cake tin with baking paper, pour in the mixture and level the top. Cook for 1 hour in a moderate oven (Gas Mark 4, 350°F, 180°C). Leave in the tin to cool.

To make the topping and filling, mix together the margarine, sugar, milk and vanilla essence. Slice the cake in two, spread in the cream and sandwich together. Spread the top and sides of the cake with apricot jam, and apply the chopped nuts to cover.

Serves 6

APRICOT AND WALNUT CAKE

50 g (2 oz) breadcrumbs
225 g (8 oz) self raising flour
2 eggs, beaten
1 tablespoon milk
175 g (6 oz) sugar
175 g (6 oz) butter or margarine
50 g (2 oz) shelled walnuts, chopped
100 g (4 oz) dried apricots, cut up small
$^1/_2$ teaspoon salt
$^1/_2$ teaspoon vanilla essence
1 teaspoon brown sugar

Cream together the sugar and the butter. Mix in the beaten eggs and the milk, then the breadcrumbs, flour, salt and vanilla essence. Beat until smooth. Add the fruit and chopped nuts. Pour into a lined cake tin and sprinkle a teaspoon of brown sugar over the top. Bake for 45 minutes in a moderate oven (Gas Mark 4, 350°F, 180°C). This cake is delicious sliced and spread with butter.

Serves 8

CAKE LOAF

50 g (2 oz) breadcrumbs
100 g (4 oz) self raising flour
175 g (6 oz) butter or margarine
175 g (6 oz) sugar
100 g (4 oz) sultanas
100 g (4 oz) mixed fruit
1 egg
3 tablespoons milk
1 teaspoon bicarbonate of soda
$1/2$ teaspoon vanilla essence

Cream together the butter and sugar and stir in the flour and the breadcrumbs. Beat the egg together with the milk, vanilla essence and bicarbonate of soda. Mix in with the other ingredients. Finally add the fruit. Line a small loaf tin with greased paper, pour in the mixture and bake in a moderate oven (Gas Mark 4, 350°F, 180°C) for 1 hour. When cold, serve slices spread with butter.

Serves 6-8

CHOCOLATE AND CARROT CAKE

50 g (2 oz) breadcrumbs
225 g (8 oz) self raising flour
1 carrot, finely grated
175 g (6 oz) sugar
2 tablespoons cooking oil
2 tablespoons cocoa
2 tablespoons milk
$\frac{1}{2}$ teaspoon bicarbonate of soda
$\frac{1}{2}$ teaspoon salt
2 eggs
3 drops vanilla essence

Mix together the carrot, breadcrumbs and sugar and stir in the oil. Whisk the eggs with the milk and vanilla essence and add to the mixture. Mix the cocoa, salt and bicarbonate of soda into the flour and sift into the bowl, mixing well. Pour the mixture into a cake tin lined with buttered paper. Bake in a medium hot oven (Gas Mark 4, 350°F, 180°C) for 1 hour. Serve warm with ice cream or leave to cool, slice in two and fill with whipped cream, spreading the top with chocolate icing.

Serves 6

CHOCOLATE TRUFFLES

175 g (6 oz) breadcrumbs

175 g (6 oz) sugar

175 g (6 oz) margarine

50 g (2 oz) ground almonds

2 dessertspoons cocoa

1 dessertspoon milk

6 drops almond essence

1 dessertspoon brandy (optional)

Melt the margarine in a saucepan and stir in the milk, sugar and cocoa. When the sugar has dissolved, remove from the heat, add the almond essence and ground almonds and stir in the breadcrumbs. Leave for a few minutes to cool, then take a teaspoonful at a time and shape into rounds on a plate. Sprinkle over each one a little ground almond and leave until completely cold.

For a special occasion, replace the milk with brandy.

Makes 30

CHRISTMAS CAKE

225 g (8 oz) self raising flour
50 g (2 oz) breadcrumbs
50 g (2 oz) brown sugar
100 g (4 oz) butter
225 g (8 oz) currants
100 g (4 oz) sultanas
100 g (4 oz) raisins
100 g (4 oz) glacé cherries
75 g (3 oz) carrot, grated
50 g (2 oz) candied peel, chopped
3 eggs
2 tablespoons milk
1 tablespoon treacle
1 tablespoon marmalade
1 teaspoon mixed spice
1 teaspoon bicarbonate of soda
juice and finely grated rind of $\frac{1}{2}$ lemon
$\frac{1}{2}$ teaspoon salt
$\frac{1}{2}$ teaspoon vanilla essence

Place into a mixing bowl all the dry ingredients and mix together with the fruit, marmalade, treacle, lemon juice and rind. Use a blender to combine the butter, sugar, eggs and milk, and add to the other ingredients in the bowl. Mix well together. Spoon into a 9-inch cake tin lined with buttered paper and cook for 1 hour in a hot oven (Gas Mark 6, 400°F, 200°C). Test by inserting a skewer. If it comes away clean, the cake is cooked.

This recipe makes a lovely dark, rich cake that is not too heavy.

Serves 10

COCONUT AND CHERRY CAKE

50 g (2 oz) breadcrumbs
100 g (4 oz) self raising flour
175 g (6 oz) white sugar
175 g (6 oz) margarine
50 g (2 oz) desiccated coconut
2 eggs
1 tablespoon milk
100 g (4 oz) glacé cherries, halved
1 teaspoon baking powder
salt

Cream the margarine and sugar together. Whisk together the eggs and milk, and fold in. Stir in the flour and the breadcrumbs, the desiccated coconut and the halved cherries. Mix well together and add a pinch of salt and baking powder. Pour into a cake tin lined with buttered paper. Cook in a moderate to hot oven (Gas Mark 5, 375°F, 190°C) for 40 minutes, then lower the temperature to Gas Mark 4, 350°F, 180°C, for the last 20 minutes. Test by pressing a finger on the top of the cake. It will spring back when cooked.

Serves 6-8

COCONUT SANDWICH

50 g (2 oz) breadcrumbs

100 g (4 oz) self raising flour

100 g (4 oz) margarine

100 g (4 oz) sugar

2 eggs, beaten

2 tablespoons milk

1 teaspoon baking powder

1 dessertspoon desiccated coconut

For the filling and topping

100 g (4 oz) margarine

100 g (4 oz) castor sugar

1 teaspoon desiccated coconut

1 tablespoon milk

4 tablespoons icing sugar

To make the cake, cream the margarine and sugar, and add the eggs and milk that have been well beaten together. Add the breadcrumbs, flour, coconut and the baking powder and mix well together. Pour the mixture into a deep sandwich cake tin, and bake for 30 minutes in a moderate oven (Gas Mark 4, 350°F, 180°C). Remove from the oven and allow to cool.

Make the filling by creaming the margarine and sugar. Mix the desiccated coconut into the milk then beat into the creamed ingredients.

Cut open the cake and spread with the filling mixture. Sandwich together. Cover with some water icing made by mixing the icing sugar with a few drops of water, or simply dredge with icing sugar and sprinkle on a little extra coconut.

Serves 6-8

COFFEE AND WALNUT CAKE

50 g (2 oz) breadcrumbs
175 g (6 oz) self raising flour
175 g (6 oz) sugar
100 g (4 oz) soft margarine
2 tablespoons milk
1 egg
1 tablespoon chopped walnuts
1 dessertspoon coffee powder
1 teaspoon baking powder
salt

Cream the margarine and sugar. Beat the egg and milk well together and stir in gradually with the dry ingredients until all are well mixed in. If the mixture seems a little too moist, add an extra tablespoon of flour. Pour into a cake tin lined with buttered paper and bake in a moderate oven (Gas Mark 4, 350°F, 180°C) for 1 hour.

Serves 8

CRUMBLE COOKIES

For the topping

50 g (2 oz) breadcrumbs
25 g (1 oz) butter
1 teaspoon almond essence

For the cookies

50 g (2 oz) breadcrumbs
100 g (4 oz) self raising flour
75 g (3 oz) butter
100 g (4 oz) sugar
2 tablespoons water
4 drops vanilla essence

First make the topping by melting the butter with the almond essence in a frying pan. Add the breadcrumbs and stir with a wooden spoon for a minute or two until crisp. Remove from pan and allow to cool.

Cream the butter and the sugar, then add the flour and the breadcrumbs, adding a little water to bind. Place in the refrigerator to go cold.

Roll out the mixture on a lightly floured board until $1/8$ inch thick. Cut into small rounds. Brush the tops with a little milk, then press on one teaspoon of the previously prepared breadcrumb topping. Space well apart on a greased baking tray and bake in a hot oven (Gas Mark 6, 400°F, 200°C) for 10 minutes. Place on a wire rack to cool.

CRUNCHY CHOCOLATE SQUARES

175 g (6 oz) breadcrumbs
175 g (6 oz) sugar
2 tablespoons cocoa
50 g (2 oz) margarine
2 tablespoons milk
3 drops vanilla essence

Place the breadcrumbs under a hot grill for a few minutes, in which time they will become golden brown and crunchy. Leave to cool.

Place all the other ingredients in a saucepan over a medium heat stirring until the sugar is dissolved. Do not allow to boil. Remove from the heat and add the breadcrumbs, mixing well in. Spread in a greased square tin or dish. Allow to cool then cut up into twelve or sixteen squares. Store in a tin.

Makes 12-16

FRUIT, NUT AND GINGER CAKE

50 g (2 oz) breadcrumbs
100 g (4 oz) sugar
100 g (4 oz) soft margarine
225 g (8 oz) self raising flour
225 g (8 oz) mixed fruit
2 eggs, beaten
120 ml (4 fluid oz) milk
1 tablespoon ground ginger
1 tablespoon mixed nuts, chopped
$^1/_2$ teaspoon baking powder

For the icing

$^1/_2$ teaspoon ground ginger
icing sugar
2 teaspoons water

Beat together the eggs with the milk. Cream the margarine and sugar, add a little flour and some of the egg mixture alternately, until all are mixed in. Add the breadcrumbs and baking powder and finally stir in the fruit, nuts and ground ginger. Pour into a cake tin lined with buttered paper and bake in a moderate to hot oven (Gas Mark 5, 375°F, 190°C) for $1\frac{1}{4}$ hours. Leave to go cold.

Mix a little icing sugar with a good pinch of powdered ginger and the water and mix into a smooth icing. Spread evenly over the top of the cake.

Serves 8-10

GINGER CAKE

50 g (2 oz) breadcrumbs
175 g (6 oz) self raising flour
100 g (4 oz) sugar
100 g (4 oz) soft margarine
1 egg
2 tablespoons milk
50 g (2 oz) crystallized ginger, chopped
1 dessertspoon orange marmalade
1 teaspoon ground ginger
1/2 teaspoon bicarbonate of soda
1/4 teaspoon salt

Cream the margarine with the sugar in a food processor, then add the egg and the milk and process until well mixed. Add the breadcrumbs, then a mixture of the flour, ground ginger, salt and bicarbonate of soda. Blend well. Finally, add the marmalade and the crystallized ginger. Spoon into a 6-inch cake tin lined with greased paper. Bake for 50 minutes in a medium to hot oven (Gas Mark 5, 375°F, 190°C).

Serves 8

GINGERBREAD

50 g (2 oz) breadcrumbs

100 g (4 oz) raisins

100 g (4 oz) self raising flour

3 tablespoons sunflower oil

100 g (4 oz) brown sugar

1 tablespoon golden syrup

1 tablespoon crystallized ginger, chopped

1 teaspoon ground ginger

1 teaspoon baking powder

1 egg

pinch of salt

Mix together the dry ingredients. Warm the syrup and oil in a saucepan and pour onto the dry ingredients, mixing well. Whisk the egg and add to the mixture. Pour into a 2 lb loaf tin lined with greased paper and bake for 1 hour in a moderate oven (Gas Mark 4, 350°F, 180°C).

GRIDDLE SCONES

50 g (2 oz) fine white breadcrumbs
100 g (4 oz) self raising flour
1 egg, beaten
120 ml (4 fluid oz) milk
1 tablespoon sugar
1 tablespoon melted butter
1 teaspoon baking powder
salt

Mix together the flour, breadcrumbs, sugar and salt. Beat together the egg and milk and add to the dry ingredients. Slowly stir in the melted butter. Finally, add the baking powder just before cooking. Drop the mixture a dessertspoonful at a time onto a lightly oiled frying pan or griddle over a low heat. Cook for a few minutes on each side.

Lemon Cake

50 g (2 oz) white breadcrumbs

100 g (4 oz) soft margarine

225 g (8 oz) self raising flour

100 g (4 oz) castor sugar

2 dessertspoons vegetable oil

2 large eggs, beaten

juice and finely grated rind of 1 lemon

1 level teaspoon baking powder

salt

For the filling

2 tablespoons raspberry jam

50 g (2 oz) margarine

75 g (3 oz) castor sugar

2 teaspoons milk

Cream together the margarine, sugar and oil, then add the breadcrumbs and the beaten

eggs. Mix well together. Mix together the baking powder, a pinch of salt and the flour and add this to the crumb mixture little by little, alternating with the lemon rind and juice.

Pour into a 6-inch cake tin lined with greased paper and bake for 45 minutes in a hot oven (Gas Mark 6, 400°F, 200°C).

Slice open the cake twice, spreading a little raspberry jam on one cut surface and some butter cream on the other. Sandwich together.

Serves 8

NUTTY SQUARES

50 g (2 oz) breadcrumbs
100 g (4 oz) self raising flour
175 g (6 oz) butter
175 g (6 oz) sugar
3 drops almond essence
1 tablespoon chopped nuts
100 g (4 oz) chocolate
2 tablespoons ground almonds

Melt the butter in a pan and gradually add the sugar, the flour and the breadcrumbs, a few drops of almond essence and the chopped nuts. Line a Swiss roll tin with greased paper and fill with the mixture, pressing down well into the corners. Cook in a medium hot oven (Gas Mark 5, 375°F, 190°C) for about 20 minutes.

While this is cooking, take a bar of chocolate (milk or plain depending on your taste) and grate it into flakes. Remove the tin from the oven and sprinkle the chocolate on while still hot. Spread the melting chocolate evenly over the top. Just before the chocolate sets, sprinkle on a little ground almond. Cut into squares while still warm.

Serves 8

OPEN MINCE TARTS

225 g (8 oz) shortcrust pastry

450 g (1 lb) jar mincemeat

50 g (2 oz) ground almonds

25 g (1 oz) breadcrumbs

3 drops almond essence

Line a mince pie tin with short crust pastry and add one teaspoonful of mincemeat to each pastry case. Mix together the ground almonds with the breadcrumbs and almond essence, then sprinkle over the mincemeat. Bake for 30 minutes in a moderate oven (Gas Mark 4, 350°F, 180°C) until golden.

Makes 12

Useful hint
Turn stale cakes or scones into a delicious sweet by cutting them up into chunks and placing in an ovenware dish. Beat together two eggs, a dessertspoon of sugar, and mix well with a pint of milk. Pour over the cake or scones and bake for 30 minutes in a moderate oven (Gas Mark 4, 350°F, 180°C).

RAISIN, CHERRY AND WALNUT CAKE

50 g (2 oz) breadcrumbs
225 g (8 oz) self raising flour
100 g (4 oz) sugar
100 g (4 oz) butter or margarine
2 eggs
120 ml (4 fluid oz) milk
50 g (2 oz) walnuts, chopped
50 g (2 oz) raisins
50 g (2 oz) glacé cherries
$1/_2$ teaspoon baking powder
$1/_2$ teaspoon vanilla essence

Cream the butter and sugar in a warm bowl and blend in a little of the flour. Whisk together the eggs and milk and add to the mixture in the bowl. Stir in the flour, breadcrumbs, baking powder and vanilla essence and lastly the raisins, nuts and cherries. Pour into a lined 6-inch cake tin and bake for 1 hour on the middle shelf at Gas Mark 4, 350°F, 180°C. Test to see if cooked by pressing with your finger. If it leaves a dent, leave in the oven a little longer.

Serves 6-8

SEED CAKE

50 g (2 oz) breadcrumbs
100 g (4 oz) self raising flour
175 g (6 oz) sugar
175 g (6 oz) soft margarine
2 eggs
2 tablespoons milk
3 drops vanilla essence
1 dessertspoon caraway seeds
1 teaspoon baking powder
1 teaspoon brown sugar

Cream the margarine and sugar in a warm bowl and add a little of the flour. Pour the eggs and milk into a blender and mix together. Add to the bowl, then gradually mix in the flour, baking powder, breadcrumbs, a few drops of vanilla essence, then the seeds, reserving a few for the top of the cake. Pour into a cake tin lined with buttered paper. Sprinkle the top of the cake with a teaspoonful of sugar and a few caraway seeds. Bake in a medium hot oven (Gas Mark 5, 375°F, 190°C) for 1 hour.

Serves 6-8

WALNUT SPICED LOAF

50 g (2 oz) breadcrumbs
175 g (6 oz) self raising flour
175 g (6 oz) soft margarine
175 g (6 oz) sugar
50 g (2 oz) chopped walnuts
1 egg, beaten
120 ml (4 fluid oz) milk
1 teaspoon mixed spice
1 teaspoon brown sugar

Cream the margarine and sugar, then add the breadcrumbs to which a dessertspoon of the flour has been added. Mix well, then add the beaten egg and milk and beat. Add the spice to the flour and stir into the mixture, adding the chopped walnuts last of all. Spoon into a lined loaf tin and sprinkle the top with a few chopped nuts and a spoonful of brown sugar. Bake for 50 minutes in a hot oven (Gas Mark 6, 400°F, 200°C).

Serves 6-8

Index